"... A person's wo[...] in what he can or cannot do, or in how he looks, or even in how he acts. Ultimately a person has worth because he is created in the image of God, because he has an eternal soul, and because God loved him enough to become a man and die for the forgiveness of that eternal soul. In the scope of eternity, nothing else really matters.

"And Tara knows this and understands it. Recently a little neighbor boy asked Tara when she was going to get well. Tara just smiled her sweet, peaceful smile and said, 'When I get to heaven, then I'll be perfect.' I don't think anyone on earth could ever boast of a more glorious future. That is true achievement of our highest potential."

TARA

Michael and Donna Nason

Foreword by Robert H. Schuller

SPIRE BOOKS

Fleming H. Revell Company
Old Tappan, New Jersey

ISBN 0-8007-8400-6
A Spire Book
Published by Fleming H. Revell Company
Originally Published by
Hawthorn Books, Inc.
Copyright © 1974, 1981 by Michael and Donna Nason
All Rights Reserved
Printed in the United States of America

Dedicated to the Glory of God
and to our children
Mark
Tara
and
Christa

Contents

Foreword

Do you have a stubborn problem that has hounded you so long you're inclined to believe it's impossible to ever solve it? Are you, in the face of dreams, opportunities, and difficulties, tempted to become an impossibility thinker and give up? Do you secretly harbor such self-deprecating thoughts as "I can't do it!" "I don't have what it takes!" "I won't succeed!"?

Does some habit have a grip on you? You've tried to break it, only to fall back into the old rut until you're ready to quit trying to break free? And for your mounting frustrations, are you on the verge of losing hope, of becoming an authentic cynic, snickering at faith and putting down possibility thinking as a phony, unrealistic, mental process of self-delusion?

Then this book will revolutionize your life!

For in these pages, you will meet a six-year-old girl whose

courage, determination, faith, and hope will shake, shatter, and crumble the very foundations of your cynicism and unbelief!

I challenge anyone to read the incredible but true accomplishments of this astounding little living doll without discovering this life-transforming revelation: "If you have faith as a grain of mustard seed, you can say to your mountain, 'move,' and nothing will be impossible to you."

Every word in this book is true. There are no exaggerations. I know. Tara is one of my very special little friends. I love her like one of my own little daughters. Her parents are my affectionate associates. My executive assistant is her dad. I'll never be more proud of any pages I write than I am of these words, which introduce the dynamic parents of this astounding miracle named Tara.

I'll never forget the first time I saw her. She was lying on her worktable wearing lavender leotards, ready for her grueling exercise, which would put to shame the greatest athletes in professional life today. Her bright eyes sparkled. Her long, walnut-colored tresses framed her beautiful twinkling face.

Precisely at the start of the minute hand she kicked off on her tough physical routine, singing a song to set a rhythm for the exercise. Her crystal-clear voice could be heard singing louder than the accompanying voices of the four neighborhood ladies, who work in rhythmic unison "patterning" Tara. Their song filled the exercise room; "Jesus loves me, this I know! . . . We are weak, but He is strong!"

It was too much for me! I had to turn away and dry my eyes, ashamed of the times I had inwardly complained about a problem, or entertained an impossibility thought.

"And a little child shall lead them," a wise man once declared. I prophesy, I predict, and I promise you that if you read this book to its last page you'll never again say, "I can't do it." "It's impossible." "God isn't real."

When you have finished the last chapter, come back and read my closing sentence. Here it is: "If Tara could solve her problems, don't you think you can make your dreams come true, too?"

ROBERT H. SCHULLER

Dr. Robert H. Schuller is founder and senior minister of Garden Grove Community Church in Garden Grove, California, and author of several best-selling books, including *Move Ahead with Possibility Thinking, Self-Love,* and *You Can Become the Person You Want to Be.* In addition, millions of Americans draw inspiration from his TV program, "Hour of Power."

Acknowledgments

This book would not be complete without sincere thanks to Kristine Tolman for her countless hours spent typing this manuscript; to Mary Gail Hobbs and Casey McDonald for continuing Tara's program while Donna and I wrote; and, of course, to several hundred dedicated people who gave unselfishly of their time to pattern Tara.

A special thank you goes to Margo Clarke, who was our pattern team coordinator for two years, and to her daily team captains, Iris Bjorklund, Wilma Chain, Esther Gash, Arlene Handren, Sharyn Manning, Sonia Scott, and Virginia Smith, who gave generously of their time to see that all of Tara's hours were filled with volunteers.

TARA

1

Happy Anniversary

The summer sun beat down relentlessly on our new green Porsche. We had the top down and were driving through the arid terrain that leads from California's Clear Lake south to what the local natives call the wine country of the Napa Valley in northern California.

It was August 10, 1970, our seventh wedding anniversary—Donna's and mine. A happy day, filled with pleasant memories and the anticipation of many good years to come. After all, we were young, fairly prosperous, and on the way up. We did the same things other young couples in our financial bracket did. We owned our own home in the suburbs, had two cars, a dog, and two children.

We were relaxed after four days of vacationing together, and feeling rather smug that day. Our children were being taken care of at the home of our friend, Mrs. Lanie Whetmore. We would spend our anniversary leisurely ambling through the wine country, then proceed to San Francisco where we planned to take an afternoon nap before going out to Ernie's, one of the city's famous restaurants, for dinner.

Yes, it was a happy day. Donna sat by my side as we wound our way through the mountain passes. At twenty-six, she was forever being mistaken for a much younger woman. People would encounter us in hotel elevators and other public places and ask: "On your honeymoon?" Donna would quickly reply, "Oh, no. I have two children, five and two," and they would laugh and say, "You look so young."

Her fair skin and blond hair glistened as the morning sun filtered through the trees overhead; her blue eyes were covered by big oval sunglasses. Donna's move to Palos Verdes Estates, California, from Houston, Texas, ten years before had taken its toll in the loss of her beautiful southern accent, which I sorely missed.

We were coming into the lush rolling hills that are characteristic of Napa Valley, where so many of our country's fine wines are produced. The vines were heavy with grapes almost ready for the autumn harvest.

We stopped at the Charles Krug Winery, where we received a long guided tour of the facilities. The two hours spent there passed quickly as we watched the fascinating process of wine making in its oldest and then in its most modern forms.

"I think I'll check in with the office," I told Donna. "Help me find a telephone."

Ahead and to our left, I spotted a phone in front of an old country store shaded by big California oak trees. It was a relaxing sight and one rarely seen in California because of the growth the state has been experiencing.

I dialed the familiar number and our office manager, Lois Lundberg, answered.

"Hi, Lois. This is Mike Nason. Yes, we're fine. Having a wonderful time. Say, do you think Vic would mind if we stayed an extra day? I promised Donna we could spend one night in San Luis Obispo on the way home. Great! We're touring the wine country now. Would you like me to bring you a bottle of champagne? Okay. Bye."

Back on the road again, I enjoyed maneuvering the car through the winding roads and hills, stopping at several more wineries as we made our way south. As we drove onto the Golden Gate Bridge leading into San Francisco, we could look out across the bay at the skyline of this, my favorite city. Each city has its own special quality, but San Francisco, with its hills and cable cars, flower stands on sidewalk corners, and quaint shops and restaurants, has a truly international flavor.

We arrived at our hotel, The Clift, around two-thirty, barely finding a place to park on the narrow, crowded street. We were hot and tired, but happy, and anxious for a cool shower and a refreshing nap before a night on the town.

Donna sat down in an easy chair in the lobby, feeling a bit out of place in her casual pants suit amidst the other women in their slightly more formal clothes. I went up to the desk and took care of the usual registration details and accepted a key to our room.

"Oh, Mr. Nason," the desk clerk said, as he handed me a slip of paper, "There's a phone message for you."

My surprise turned to shocked concern as I read the note:

Call Lanie Whetmore at Children's Hospital of Orange County 714-633-6030.

My mind raced as I folded the memo and tucked it into my shirt pocket. "One of the children," I thought, icy fingers clutching at my throat. I decided not to tell Donna until we were settled in our room. It was a lovely one, decorated in shades of blue, with some fine antique pieces of furniture. I tried to act naturally, but Donna instinctively sensed my sudden change of mood.

"What's the matter, Michael?" she asked, as soon as the bellhop had left us alone.

"Sit down, Donna," was all I said.

"Why? What's wrong?" she asked, concern rising in her voice.

"When I registered, there was a message for us. Here it is," I said, passing the note to her.

Her face flushed crimson as she read its contents. "Oh," she said, trying to sound unconcerned. "Maybe Mark broke his arm."

"Somehow I don't think so," I said, "I have a funny feeling about it." I could feel perspiration running through my hair and down my back.

Trembling, we both went to the phone. A hundred thoughts were tumbling through my mind. Which one is it? What has happened? I wondered silently.

I pictured our two children, so very dear to us. There was Mark, our five-year-old. I could see his tawny hair and big blue eyes with gold flecks in them, his skin brown and shining from the California sun. I thought of how much I loved him, and of the problems we had in relating to him. Probably the most active youngster in the neighborhood, he was hyperkinetic and had some learning disabilities. This fall he would not be going to the neighborhood school to kindergarten. Donna would be driving him thirty miles away to

Orange, as she had done last year, so that he could receive special education.

Then my thoughts shifted to Tara, our baby. She had just turned two on July 2. She was our sunshine, and I had often wondered how we had ever managed before this ever-smiling, delightful child came into our lives. Her wavy dark-brown hair had just grown long enough for two ponytails, and her laughing blue eyes were rimmed with dark curly lashes.

"I wonder which one it is," Donna repeated over and over. I jiggled the phone nervously, but it was dead.

"There's one in the hall by the elevators," Donna said.

We were running now, our anxiety growing by the minute. I grabbed clumsily for the receiver, but it, too, was silent.

"Wait! I remember, the last time I was here, there was a telephone in the bathroom."

We raced back inside. Sure enough, there was a phone in this highly unlikely place. I sat on the commode lid to dial. Donna was huddled over me, her eyes filled with fear and uncertainty. We waited breathlessly as I dialed the hotel switchboard. It seemed forever before the operator came on the line.

"This is Mr. Nason in Room 721. I'd like to call Children's Hospital in Orange County."

"Oh, Mr. Nason. We've been waiting for you all day. I'll get the number for you; then I'll stay on the line in case you need me."

"Thank you," I replied.

The knowledge of the operator's awareness of the urgency of the message made me believe she knew what lay ahead on this long distance call. However, possibly from fear, I didn't ask her what was wrong or what she knew of the events leading up to this moment.

As we both waited for the hospital to answer, the suspense was almost unbearable. Finally, the crisp voice of the hospital operator came on the line.

"I'd like to page Mrs. Lanie Whetmore, please."

Another eternity passed before the operator came back on the line. "I'm sorry. No one has answered your page."

By this time, I was quite red in the face and beginning to lose my patience. With unbelievable self-control, I said, "This is Mr. Nason. One of my children is being treated in your hospital. My wife and I are in San Francisco. Please connect me with someone who can give me some information."

More minutes passed in that tiny bathroom before a man's voice came over the telephone.

"Mr. Nason, this is Dr. John Gibson. We have been looking for you for hours. Your child has had a serious accident."

"What kind of an accident?" I demanded almost harshly, my voice choking with alarm. Donna was virtually jumping up and down beside me.

"We don't know," Dr. Gibson replied.

"Which one? Which one?" Donna was practically screaming.

"Which child is it?" I asked.

"It's your daughter, Tara," came the answer.

I whispered to Donna, "It's Tara."

"Tara," she repeated dryly. We felt as if we were having a terrible nightmare from which we would never awaken. It just kept going on and on. . . .

"Your daughter was admitted last night around ten in grave condition, with a severe head injury. It was touch and go all night. Dr. Merle Carson, our chief of staff here, and I had to accept responsibility for her treatment since there was no note of consent from you. Her condition is currently stable. We are concerning ourselves with balancing her chemistry. I suggest that you come home as soon as possible."

I told the doctor we would take the earliest available plane out of San Francisco for Orange County.

My father then got on the line, expressed the gravity of the situation there, and said he would pick us up at the airport. We said good-bye, and the phone clicked dead. I still held the receiver in my hand, not wanting to believe what I had just heard.

The silence was broken by the hotel operator. "Mr. Nason, are you still there?"

"Yes!" I replied, not really sure of anything at that point.

"Is there anything we can do for you?"

"Yes. Would you please send us a doctor?"

"Of course, Mr. Nason. The hotel manager and security director are also on their way to your room to see what they can do to help."

I thanked her and hung up.

I don't recall why I had requested a doctor. Perhaps I expected to faint or something. I guess it's a reflex reaction in a moment of stress. There was a knock on the door. The manager and the security director identified themselves. They asked if they could help us get home.

My mind was spinning, but I managed to collect my wits enough to request plane tickets on the next flight on Air California from San Francisco to Orange County airport. The security director took charge of our car and had it stored. An hour in a hotel room had triggered a terrifying chain of events to follow. We must have looked quite a sight. The manager and security director carried our bags through the lobby to a waiting cab.

Once inside the taxi, Donna and I both broke down. The tide of tears we had been holding back through an hour of anguish now gushed forth. We could do nothing but cling to each other and cry.

"Why? Oh, why?" we kept asking. "Why our dear little Tara?" Surely a sweeter child never lived! Why should this happen to our baby? She's only two years old. "Why?" And in the back of my mind I kept thinking—brain damage, that's what you get from head injuries. No! No! Not our Tara!

Donna sobbed uncontrollably all the way home on the plane. Fortunately, it was only an hour flight. The stewardess asked if there was anything she could do to help us, and I told her we had left San Francisco so fast we hadn't had time to call my folks and tell them what plane we were on. She jotted down the information about my dad's name and the name of the hospital and took it to the pilot. When we were in range of Orange County airport, the pilot radioed the message to the field and they in turn called my father.

All the way back, Donna kept praying, "Please, God, please don't let my baby die! Please don't let Tara die!" We felt our own physical health and strength being drained in a transference to her, to help her live. And all the while we kept wondering, "Can this really be happening to us?"

I glanced at my watch. It was four-fifteen. Through her tears, Donna said, "Mike, seven years ago today at this very time we were walking down the aisle."

"I know. Happy anniversary."

"Yeah."

2

The Chase

The touchdown at Orange County airport was smooth. Numbly, we walked down the steps from the plane. As we reached the bottom, the stewardess who had been so nice during the flight caught up with us to ask if she could drive us to the hospital. But, through the blur of my tears, I spotted my father. The grim look on his face was in direct contrast to the still-warm sun. A tall man, his gray hair thinning, Dad is always in control of the situation, his blue eyes looking confidently through his glasses. But today he was deeply shaken, trying to be his usual controlled self but not succeeding very well. Our tear-stained faces made quite a sight in the midst of the happy vacationers who comprised the bulk of our fellow passengers.

"I just can't understand what happened, Dad," I said as we walked to the baggage area. "Do you know?"

"Well, I don't know very much, but I'll tell you what I can." He launched into the incredible tale. "Last night Tara wouldn't eat her dinner. She hadn't eaten or slept well since you left and had spent five hours at the beach yesterday. Lanie said Tara looked exhausted, and that she had dark circles under her eyes. Lanie decided to stop trying to get her to eat and go ahead and put her to bed.

"As she was changing her into her nightgown, Tara began to gag. Lanie, thinking she must still have a french fry in her mouth, stuck her finger in to retrieve it. But there was nothing there. It was then she realized that Tara had stopped breathing.

"She gathered her up and ran next door to her neighbor who administered mouth-to-mouth resuscitation while Lanie called the local fire department. A rescue squad responded to the call and administered oxygen. Realizing she was a very sick little girl, they called an ambulance to transport her to the hospital."

"Was she conscious?"

"I think so, but apparently there had been some seizure activity."

With that revelation, my eyes filled with tears and a heavy lump settled in my heart. I turned and walked toward the baggage area to regain my composure. I tried with all my energy to hold back the tears, my body shaking. Then I took a deep breath, turned, and walked back to Donna and my Dad. We silently retrieved our bags and got into the car. I broke the silence by asking about Mark.

"Oh, he's fine," Dad responded. "Tucker came down this morning, picked up Mark and took him home with him."

"Oh, good." I was relieved. I knew my brother Tucker and my sister-in-law Nancy would take good care of Mark.

Donna asked, "Where was Mark? Did he see Tara convulse?"

"No," Dad said. "As far as I know, he and the other children were still at Lanie's house. Tara was taken by ambulance to Tustin Community Hospital and admitted to their emergency room. They took a series of full body X rays in an attempt to find out what was wrong. That's when they discovered that Tara's skull was fractured."

"Her skull was fractured?" My voice rose to a scream. "But how? When? We spoke to Lanie about six-thirty last night. We called to tell her we had changed hotels in Clear Lake, and to see how the kids were. She said everything was fine."

"I can't understand it. Tara is so graceful and coordinated. She's never even had a skinned knee," Donna interrupted.

"Nobody seems to know how it happened, but it all started about seven-fifteen last night," Dad continued. "Anyway, I guess her condition was worsening, and the people at Tustin Community Hospital didn't feel they had the facilities to care for her, so another ambulance transported her to Children's Hospital. By this time, it was about ten o'clock at night, and Tara was slipping in and out of consciousness."

Dad adjusted his glasses carefully and looked me straight in the eye. "I think you should be aware that Children's Hospital has called in the police."

"The police? Why?"

"Apparently it is standard procedure when a child is admitted in such bad shape and there is no suitable explanation as to how it happened."

"I still don't understand why we weren't notified last night while all this was going on."

"Believe me, the people at the hospital tried. They called

and called your hotel in Clear Lake, but the clerk kept saying you weren't registered."

"But we were registered! We were there all night! I can't imagine! Oh, no!"

I gasped as I realized what had happened. We hadn't registered under our own name. We had used the credit card issued to the owner of my company (Pat Moriarty, Pyrotronics Corporation, Manufacturer of Red Devil Fireworks), and registered as Mr. and Mrs. Pat Moriarty. And we didn't even think! We had called Lanie especially to let her know about the change in our itinerary and had forgotten to tell her what name we had used!

"Oh, that's terrible!" Donna cried after I had told her. "No wonder they couldn't reach us!"

"They kept trying all night," Dad continued. "They even sent the local police out to the hotel, but they couldn't get hold of you. Then this morning the police went to both places—the motel where you had checked in originally and the one you actually stayed in. But they couldn't find you."

Donna's face was ashen. "If we had only known. Imagine all this going on while we were playing miniature golf and having such a good time. I can't believe it."

"Lanie knew you worked for Red Devil Fireworks, so they called there this morning. Your secretary gave them Tucker's number, so they called him."

"Then Tucker was the first in the family to know about it. Did he call you, Dad?"

"He made an attempt, but I had already left for work, so he talked to your mother."

"What about my parents?" Donna wanted to know. "Lanie had their number. Why weren't they notified?"

"The hospital tried to, but your folks must have gone

out of town for the weekend. No one has been home there."

"So they still don't know about Tara?"

"Not that I know of. After your secretary called Tuck, she talked to Lois Lundberg. Lois said she had just spoken with you on the phone and that you were in the wine country."

I couldn't help thinking that had we phoned Lois a little later we would have learned of the tragedy earlier. But I really don't know what good it would have done us. We still would have had that long drive to San Francisco to catch a plane. Knowing how long that hour plane ride seemed, I can only imagine the agony several hours by car would have been.

Dad was continuing his account of the day's bizarre events. "Highway patrolmen were then dispatched in the Napa area to try to locate you by car. They stopped off at several wineries to inquire, but were always about fifteen minutes behind you. Also, one of the men from your office—Leo Crawford, I think—was vacationing on Clear Lake and was standing by with his plane. As soon as the California Highway Patrol found you, he was going to fly you to San Francisco to catch a plane for Orange County," Dad continued. "There has been a big search going on for you."

I wondered what the people at the wineries must have thought when they learned that the police were looking for us. They probably thought we were some present-day version of Bonnie and Clyde.

By this time, we were rounding the corner of the hospital parking lot. Our hearts were racing, our throats dry. Our eyes had that glazed look that comes when one has cried until there is not a tear left. We were quiet now, trying to take in what had been said, mulling it all over in our minds, seeking to make some sense out of it.

Then we were in the elevator going up to the third floor and walking down the corridor toward the intensive care unit. Walking slowly, heavily, like two people in a dream—afraid to hear what must be heard and afraid not to. Outside the elevator sat Lanie, our friend and baby-sitter, wearing a swimsuit and wrapped in a hospital blanket. She had not left the hospital since their hurried arrival the night before. Her normal active young self was gone.

She blinked at us and repeated nervously over and over, "Oh, Tara looks so much better today than she did last night."

Dad spoke to a nurse, who glanced at us sympathetically and promptly disappeared. She returned with a young man of about our age. He was unshaven and looked exhausted, his dark hair and white coat disheveled. His outstretched hand indicated that he expected me to shake it. Automatically I did.

"Mr. and Mrs. Nason," he said, "I'm Dr. Gibson. Why don't we step into this room where we can talk." He apologized for his appearance, explaining that he had not left Tara's side since her admittance twenty hours earlier, even though his own daughter of about the same age was down the hall suffering from an acute case of pneumonia. The three of us drew up chairs in a small room off the corridor.

With his hands clasped before him, Dr. Gibson leaned toward us and, in a confidential manner, started his report of the day just past. "Tara's had a rough time of it. She's still not out of the woods and won't be for some time to come. We've really had to work at balancing her blood chemistries to keep her alive."

"Is she . . . in a coma?" I could barely form the words and was scared to death to hear the answer. All I could think of was a Dr. Kildare episode on TV where a man slipped and fell alongside a swimming pool, lapsed into a coma, and never regained consciousness. His brother finally murdered him to put the family out of their misery. That was really about all I knew about comas.

Dr. Gibson stared down at his hands. "Yes, she is in a comatose state."

Donna and I looked at each other, our eyes silently pleading for help; seeking to share in some way the infinite sorrow and despair that was welling up inside and getting ready to spill over.

He started to outline Tara's problems and what was being done to save her life.

"When Tara arrived here last night she was in a semi-comatose state. She suffered a seizure in the emergency room. We ordered X rays, which revealed an occipital skull fracture. This means that the lower base of the skull is fractured. We have also noted that she has retinal hemorrhages in both eyes. The bruises that you will see on her body are common in persons who have suffered severe brain injury. All we can do at the moment is balance her body chemistry so that she can survive the trauma she experienced."

He paused a moment, then added, "I've ordered a sedative for each of you."

He handed each of us a little white pill and a cup of water. We swallowed them mechanically, each privately wondering if a little white pill could mend a broken heart.

"We've called in numerous specialists on the case," he went on. "Your pediatrician, a neurosurgeon, an orthopedist, a cardiologist, and an opthalmologist. They are all considered tops in their fields." Again he paused, this time looking intently at both of us. "Would you like to see your daughter?"

We glanced back at him blankly and a little fearfully.

"You've got to face it sooner or later," he said.

He led us to an area next door to the intensive care unit and explained that we could go into the unit for five minutes out of each hour around the clock. He showed us where to scrub our hands and how to put on the green gowns, hats, and masks that had to be worn in the room.

Then we timidly tiptoed into the room and over to the bed where Tara lay. We really didn't know what to expect, but the sight that met our eyes was even worse than we had imagined. Tara had always slept in a crib at home, and the standard-size hospital bed made her lifeless body look even more tiny and helpless.

When we had left her—could it be only five days before—she had been full of summer's glow, tan and healthy and rosy-cheeked, with the proverbial lively smile on her face. This Tara was thin, almost emaciated-looking, and just as white as the sheet on which she was lying. Her mouth was partially open and held a motionless grimace as though she were in pain. Her lips were exceedingly dry and chapped. Her sparkling blue eyes were expressionless, half closed, and unblinking. Her breathing was labored and slow. She lay naked and completely immobile on the bed. Not a muscle stirred. She seemed to have tubes and wires taped all over her and needles stuck into her skin at various places, attached to different intravenous containers. There was a catheter leading to a plastic bag filled with urine. A bedside TV unit monitored her heart.

As we gazed down at our beautiful baby, the pain that we felt was indescribable. It was deep and searing and penetrated down to the very marrow of our bones. It hurt too badly for tears. The sadness clung to us like a suit of heavy armor that we couldn't shake off. I had heard of people carrying heavy burdens, and I felt this must be exactly the feeling: a load too great to bear, dragging us down to the depths of despair.

Even as we looked at Tara's bruised little body, our minds couldn't quite grasp the full magnitude of the situation. It seemed so utterly incredible.

"Tara, Tara," Donna whispered softly in her ear. "It's Mommy. Mommy and Daddy are here. We love you, Tara."

"Tara, Daddy's here," I said. "Everything's going to be all right."

In our minds, we didn't really expect an answer. But our hearts were longing to see some glimpse of recognition, no matter how small, on her still little face. But there was only silence, deadly silence. Finally a nurse came and led us out of the room and back into the brightly lit hospital corridor.

3

Ninety-nine—Ninety-nine

I saw that my mother had now joined my dad in the hospital waiting room, and Donna and I went forward to give her a hug. Mother is an attractive woman in her fifties, with blue eyes and frosted brown hair. She gave us a weak smile and fumbled for the right words of consolation. The tranquilizers had begun to take effect, and between that and the grief we felt we were utterly weary and defeated. It was all we could do to put one foot in front of the other, much less carry on a conversation.

After sitting quietly for a while, Donna's mother and father, Doug and Claire Henson, were ushered into the room. They are a handsome couple. Donna's dad has a full head of wavy gold hair and blue eyes staring from behind his glasses. He is short and rather stout and his skin is tan from constant exposure to the California sun. Her mother's face was tear-streaked. She was deeply shaken.

Donna's mother was one of the most easygoing people I had ever known, attractive and youthful like her daughter. They hurried toward us, their shaky embraces betraying the depth of their emotion. Kaki and Bob DeWalt, dear friends since high school days, joined us shortly thereafter and stayed to watch and wait with us.

We made quite a pathetic little family group that night, pacing up and down the halls. For five minutes out of each hour, Donna and I would enter the intensive care unit to see Tara, hoping and praying each time to detect some glimmer of life. But each time she looked just the same. We finally summoned enough courage to caress her frail little body, but our touch set the monitoring devices to quivering so much that it frightened us, and we quickly withdrew our hands.

Near midnight Dr. Eugene Ronar, Mark and Tara's pediatrician, strode into the waiting room. A tall, youngish man with tired blue eyes, he ran his hands through his thinning dark blond hair.

"We've just been going over Tara's X rays," he said, "and we've discovered a fracture in her lower left arm."

"Her arm is broken?" I half-screamed and shook my head in disbelief. "I can't understand! How could she have a broken arm?"

"I don't know," Dr. Ronar said rather cynically, "but it looks like she fell off a cliff."

"Are you going to put a cast on it?" I asked.

"No," he said. "Because she has no movement anyway, we will just splint it."

Donna and I went home around one o'clock and riffled through the mail that had accumulated during our five-day absence. The anniversary cards reminded us of the carefree couple we had been yesterday. It seemed funny that the outside world went on, even though our own little world had crumbled. Several of our neighbors had seen lights on at our house and came over to welcome us home. In a small town like Mission Viejo news travels fast, and they all had heard about Tara. They were anxious to know how she was, and told us they were praying for her.

We were exhausted and with the sedative Dr. Gibson had prescribed, we fell asleep quickly. But our sleep was fitful and shallow. We awoke at intervals and always our thoughts returned to Tara and to the bizarre events of the day. We found ourselves dreading the ring of the telephone. There was the constant fear that any call might bring news that Tara had died.

We awoke the next morning still tired, and with a heavy feeling in the bottom of our stomachs. I called the hospital right away and was told that Tara's condition was "stable." How often we were to hear that word, and how little it really meant.

We dressed mechanically that morning. I guess we were just kind of numb. Donna was drawn to Tara's bedroom, which was right next to ours. She kept going in there that day and for many others to come, just standing in the doorway, looking, with tears streaming down her face. It is a terrible thing to see your wife like that, wanting so desperately to help her, yet having nothing to offer but your own despair.

Donna wanted to take to the hospital a portrait of Tara that had been taken the previous Christmas. In it, she and Mark were dressed in matching blue sailor suits. "Just so the doctors and nurses will know what she's really like," she said.

When we got to the hospital that morning, we were questioned by two police investigators, who were trying to find out what had happened to Tara. We told them all we could about Tara, her personality and habits. We explained to them what a sweet, happy little girl she was, about how extremely coordinated and graceful she was. We just couldn't imagine her having an accident that hurt her in such a dreadful way.

On the other hand, we told them that the baby-sitter, Lanie, was a respected and trusted friend, who had given us no cause for concern in the year and a half we had known her. She had watched Mark and Tara for us many times, with never a problem. Her husband is a career Marine, who was out of the country that year, and she was devoted to him.

The police investigated for several days; and Donna and I questioned Lanie and the parents of other children who were there that fateful weekend. To our extreme disappointment, no one was able to come up with any concrete facts as to how Tara could have suffered such extensive injuries. If she had fallen and somehow struck her head during play, no one had seen it—and Tara had not told Lanie or anyone else of having fallen or having hurt herself.

The fact that Tara's accident was a mystery was hard to accept. We were never to know what actually happened to her. It seemed especially difficult for friends and relatives to understand. Most of Donna's family lives in Texas, and they were quite incensed because they thought we weren't telling them all we knew. We had a difficult time explaining to them that we really didn't know anything.

The doctors said there was no way of pinpointing exactly how Tara's accident had occurred. The fact was that Tara was badly injured; it didn't really make much difference how or why. The issue was—what was going to happen to Tara, and how were we, as a family, going to cope with it?

Donna and I were not a religious couple, but we did

believe in God as a Supreme Being. We began to turn to Him for comfort. My mother had been president of the Episcopal Churchwomen in Palos Verdes Estates, California. Being friends with the pastor of the church, the Reverend Robert Tourigney, she prevailed upon him to visit us at the hospital.

He was an austere former Bostonian. He had married Donna and me, and we liked and trusted him. Somehow we felt safe when he was around, and were pleased that he took the time to make the hour's journey by car from the Palos Verdes area down to the hospital. He didn't really say much that day, just prayed with us and assured us that Tara would go to Heaven if she died. Donna and I didn't really believe there was a Heaven, but it was a comfort to hear him speak of it in such a confident way.

Later that day (August 12), the doctors decided to take Tara down to radiology for a series of skull X rays. My mother and I went downstairs to the lobby to call my sister Lynn, who lives in Las Vegas. While I was on the phone, my mother began tapping wildly on the booth. As I turned, I saw that her face had gone white. I quickly finished the conversation and came out, that now-familiar shiver going up and down my spine.

"What is it?" I demanded.

"I think there's something wrong in radiology. They just sounded 'ninety-nine' over the PA system for radiology and doctors are rushing down the hall right now. Mike, you go there and I'll run upstairs to get Donna's folks."

I began to rush toward radiology. When I reached it, I saw that my dad had gotten there ahead of me.

"It's Tara," he said. "The doctor told me to take you back upstairs. He'll be up as soon as he can."

We were both shaking as we went back up on the elevator. My mother was there, white and gasping. It seemed that because of the emergency call she had been unable to use the elevator and had run up all four flights of stairs. With her asthmatic heart, she was quite breathless.

Dr. Gibson had told her, "This is a children's hospital; we don't want grandmothers getting sick." He examined her and had to administer medication.

We were all gathered together now—my parents, Donna's parents, Reverend Tourigney, and myself. Donna was still in the waiting room reading a book, totally unaware that the "ninety-nine" call was the hospital's code for "emergency— life or death—all doctors come immediately." And she was also unaware that the call was for Tara.

Dr. Richard Coster, a neurosurgeon, soon appeared. "It's all right. We nearly lost Tara down in radiology, but she's breathing again now." We all decided it would be best not to tell Donna of Tara's narrow escape.

The next time we went in to see Tara, there was a three-inch silver cross taped to the metal head of her bed. The nurses told us it had been put there by one of the sisters who served at St. Joseph's, the adjoining Catholic hospital. They said the sisters were praying for Tara daily.

That afternoon, Dr. Coster came to me. He spoke quietly and with conviction: "We've got to relieve the pressure on Tara's brain or else she is not going to make it. We need your permission to perform burr-hole surgery. By this, I mean that we will go in and make four incisions in her scalp. Then we will drill four holes through the skull. We are hoping to find a blood clot that can be removed, thus relieving pressure. We will prepare her this evening and operate around eight-thirty. If you would like, we've made arrangements for you and your wife to spend the night in the hospital recovery room so you can be close-by if you are needed."

As I went to tell Donna, I felt somewhat relieved. At least, there was now something to do, some action to be taken. Maybe this would be the turning point; maybe Tara would come out of her coma. I was unprepared for Donna's re-action. For the first time since Monday, she really broke down and began crying hysterically.

"They're going to shave off my baby's hair!" she screamed. "I can't stand it! I can't stand it!"

She was sobbing uncontrollably, not caring who saw or heard her. This was very uncharacteristic of Donna, who is somewhat shy and keeps her feelings closely guarded. I was unable to quiet her. Finally the long-suffering Dr. Gibson spent an hour talking to her before she began to calm down.

The news spread, and that evening all of our family who lived nearby were on hand. There were both Donna's parents and mine; my sister Gale and her husband Jack Lovrich; Kaki and Bob DeWalt; and my brother Tucker. Tucker's wife Nancy was home with their three girls and our son Mark.

Donna and I went in to see Tara one last time before they shaved her head. The nurses had braided her long thick hair that morning and had even tied ribbons in it. Donna stood tall and straight, making the most of her 5'3½". Only her quivering lips and her eyes, spilling over with tears, betrayed the depth of her emotion. She was really heartsick. She didn't want Tara to have to endure surgery, but was helpless to stop it.

An attendant and several nurses prepared the equipment around Tara for transportation to surgery. They wheeled her out of the intensive care unit on her bed, and we walked by her side as our parents and other family members stood by mutely—none of us able to say or do anything to help this dear little girl. As the elevator door shut and separated us from our only daughter, I was praying fervently that surgery would make Tara better.

The big clock on the wall of the recovery room kept ticking away the minutes. Really, it seemed as though that night would go on forever. A strange hush had fallen over the room, as if sound would break the spell and somehow snip the thin golden thread of life for Tara. First we sat, then we stood, and finally we paced up and down.

Shortly after ten, Dr. Coster strode into the room. He was still wearing his green surgical garb and looked almost as weary as the rest of us. I don't suppose he was looking forward to the family inquisition that was about to begin.

He painstakingly explained the surgery once again, and finished by saying that the operation had not been successful. His studied tone couldn't quite hide his disappointment.

"We had hoped to find one or more large blood clots," he said. "Then we would have been able to remove them and reduce cerebral pressure, maybe even bring Tara out of coma. But instead we found swelling—swelling everywhere— a massive hemorrhaging that we were unable to remedy. There was nothing to do but sew her back up. I'm afraid we've done about all we can. The rest is up to Tara. She's a brave little girl with a strong will to live. She's putting up a good fight."

One by one, the family began filing out, leaving Donna and me alone in the partially darkened room. We summoned our courage and went in to see Tara. It was late now, and deathly quiet; most of the hospital was asleep. A night nurse glanced up from her desk as we tiptoed into the room; then recognizing us, she turned back to her work.

Tara looked tiny and frail, her skin translucent and color-less. Her sweet little face was all but enshrouded in a large white bandage that had been wound around her head like a turban. My eyes stung with tears as I thought of the wounds beneath the gauze, of the innocent little head shaved bald for an unsuccessful operation.

Donna had brought an Episcopal Book of Common Prayer from home that morning. It was sitting on the bedside table next to Tara's picture. Together we read silently through the pages of prayers entitled "Visitation of the Sick." Then we went back to the recovery room and prepared for bed. We were speaking in hushed tones, wondering if a nurse would awaken us during the night to tell us that our little girl was gone.

We were jarred out of a restless sleep at six o'clock in the morning by a nurse saying they would need the recovery room soon for early morning surgery patients. We rose groggily and somehow managed to get dressed.

Donna was so exhausted that she lay down on the couch in the waiting room outside the intensive care unit. As she dozed, I paced the corridor, stealing glances at Tara through the small glass window in the door leading to where she lay. At six-thirty a call over the hospital PA system sent an elec-tric shock through my body. As a woman's voice called— "ninety-nine—ninety-nine ICU," I knew that all available doctors were wanted in the intensive care unit because there existed a life-or-death situation. Somehow I sensed without being told that Tara was now dying and her struggle for life had ended. My heart raced as my feet tried to go in separate directions at the same time. My legs were like rubber. My whole body shook as I debated in my mind whether or not to look through the glass window in the door that would give me a glimpse of Tara.

Suddenly, the elevator door slid open and a doctor in a white coat hurried past and through the door into the ICU. I found myself following him, not sure I wanted to know or see what was happening on the other side of the wall. I glanced through the window and there was no question that Tara had been the object of the "ninety-nine" call.

I couldn't see Tara, due to the countless white-coated doctors and nurses who huddled around her bedside. The only sight I obtained of her frail body was that of a doctor pressing the palms of his two hands against Tara's chest as he strove to bring life back to her heart. This was more than I could tolerate. I turned away and tears filled my eyes once more, for I was fearfully certain that the battle was over— Tara had died. I paced outside the ICU wondering whether to go inside or just wait. As the minutes passed, I couldn't understand why the doctors didn't come out and tell me about Tara—what had gone wrong—and that she had passed away.

Abruptly, the door opened and Dr. Gibson emerged from the ICU and told me that Tara had had a close call. She had stopped breathing. It had been detected by the nurse on the heart-monitoring device that was attached to Tara's body and to a TV screen and an alarm.

When her heart started to fail, the nurse sounded the "ninety-nine" call. Doctors responded and administered external heart massage, and she regained her heartbeat. They put her on a respirator, a machine that would do the breathing for her. My mind was swimming.

Why couldn't there be some definitive direction in Tara's fight? Why didn't she just wake up—or die? The mental anguish was becoming more than I could bear.

Donna and I continued that now-familiar ritual of washing and putting on gowns so that we could see her. She looked just the same, a tiny, still figure on white sheets. Her bandaged head forced our minds to focus on the events of the night before.

I quickly noticed the new apparatus that had been added to the various machines keeping Tara alive. It had a nozzle that fitted in her mouth, with a hoselike device leading to the machine itself. It had a section rather like an accordian that was going in and out, at the same time making a swishing sound.

This was the respirator Dr. Gibson had told me about a few minutes before. Tara had finally stopped breathing altogether and needed this device to do the job for her. The only life function that remained was her heartbeat. She seemed to be nine-tenths in the grave, her hands losing their grasp as they tried valiantly to hold on, to keep from falling all the way into the pit.

Donna and I didn't speak of it, but we both felt the end was very near. We virtually dragged ourselves through the day, forcing ourselves through sheer will power to eat, and to speak with the friends and relatives who came once more to keep vigil with us.

Tara delights in showing off her ability to balance herself on her hands and knees. (*Photo by Mary Gail Hobbs*)

A little friendly sibling rivalry as Tara and Mark argue over which one crawls best. (*Photo by Richard and Linda Payne*)

Tara crawls down the stairs. *(Photo by Richard and Linda Payne)*

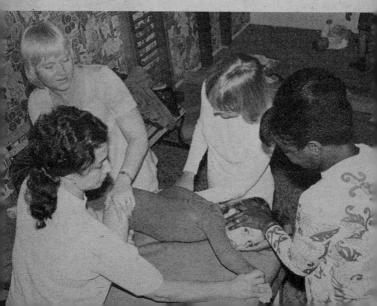

Tara sitting Indian-style while masking. (*Photo by Richard and Linda Payne*)

Tara being patterned by her volunteers.
(*Photo by Richard and Linda Payne*)

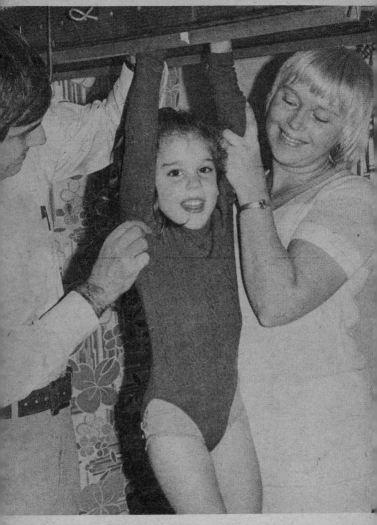

Mom and Dad help Tara to hang by her arms from her horizontal ladder. (*Photo by Richard and Linda Payne*)

Tara and her baby sister Christa. (*Photo by Richard and Linda Payne*)

Tara's fifth birthday party. (*Photo by Mary Gail Hobbs*)

Tara hangs upside down. (*Photo by Mary Gail Hobbs*)

"Snowball! What are you doing on my bed?" (*Photo by Richard and Linda Payne*)

Our Christmas angel. (*Photo by Richard and Linda Payne*)

4

Child of Light

Sometime during that afternoon, Dr. Coster drew me aside. I studied his face to see if I could detect what manner of news he might have for me. His jaw was set tight, his features were at once pensive and grim.

"Due to the recent heart transplants, new legislation has been enacted regarding legal death," he said quietly. "When a patient has reached the point of total dependence upon machines, as Tara has," he paused, groping for words, "there may come a time when the brain is functionally dead, with no hope of its performing on even the lowest level, though the patient's heart is still beating. At this time, it is legal and advisable for the life-giving machines to be turned off, thus allowing the heart to stop. It is my professional opinion that Tara is rapidly approaching this state, and that she should reach it sometime within the next twenty-four

31

hours. It is my recommendation that at that time you and Donna consider taking the action necessary to authorize us to discontinue the machines."

"Well, this is it," I thought to myself. I sucked in my breath, bit my tongue, and blinked my eyes several times. "All right, Dr. Coster," I heard my voice say. "Whatever you think best. You let me know when."

My eyes were a blur, my entire head was throbbing. What a decision to make! I shook my head in disbelief. My brain was so dulled by the four days of anguish that it could scarcely assimilate the full implications of Dr. Coster's recommendations. I talked it over with my father and Bob Tourigney, and we decided not to tell Donna until it became absolutely necessary. If we could spare her even a few hours of this additional burden, it would be worth it.

Donna, however, being a sensitive, intelligent person, sensed that I wasn't telling her all I knew.

"Look," she said, "I'm your wife. I married you because I wanted to share your life. Tara is my daughter as well as yours, and I love her just as much. You must tell me what is going on."

I stood firm about not mentioning the machines, but I did confide that I thought Tara's struggle was drawing to a close—and that she was going to lose.

Later that night, in the privacy of our home, Donna and I talked about Tara. We spoke of her funeral and what we wanted it to be like.

"I want her to wear her Easter dress," Donna said. I know she was thinking, as I was, of the sunny little girl in her yellow Easter dress. She had looked like a decorated Easter egg when she wore it. It had a white pinafore decorated with yellow flocked daisies over a yellow dress, and a coat and sunbonnet to match. Donna had taken such delight in dressing up our little daughter. "The bonnet will cover her bald head," Donna murmured through her tears.

The next morning I awoke to find that Donna was up before me. I could hear her crying softly and followed the sound. She was in Tara's room, sitting in the rocking chair where she had cuddled Tara so many times before. She was holding a big stuffed doll, her head buried in its hair, sobbing. I don't know how long I stood there before she noticed me. When she did, she spoke not a word but rose and handed me a piece of paper torn from a steno pad and walked from the room. On it was a poem she had written. The ink was stained in several places with tears. This is what it said:

Little Tara, child of light
     We love you.
     You have been our strength
        and our consolation.
     You have brought joy to all who
        have known you.
     You were my angel, but you were
        God's angel first,
     Lent to us for a short while.
     And when your job was
     Done, God has taken you back.

     We love you, we cherish you,
     We mourn for you. We live for
     Your memory. God bless you,
     My blessed angel.

As we were dressing, the doorbell rang. It was our next-door neighbor, Elaine Gover. She is an attractive woman in her early forties, the mother of three teen-aged children.

Tara had reminded her of her own daughter Diane, who was then eighteen, and she was quite fond of her. She reminded us that they were members of the Reform Church of Jesus Christ of Latter Day Saints.

"In the Bible," she said, "it says that when someone is in need of healing let the elders of the church come and anoint him with oil and pray for him. Would you mind if the elders from our church were to do this for Tara?"

"No, we would be very pleased." Donna and I responded.

"I will call them," she said. "They will fast and pray for three days before they come. Also, could I have a snapshot of Tara for the church bulletin board so the people can see for whom they are praying?"

We got her a photo taken of Tara at her second birthday party, just a month earlier. It was a picture of a happy little girl, with twinkling blue eyes and long brown hair blowing in the breeze as she looked at the cake with two candles on it. My heart sank as I thought of the Tara who was lying motionless and expressionless in a hospital bed. They really weren't the same little girl at all.

When we got to the hospital, there was nothing to do but to sit and wait. But Donna seemed different, somehow, more at peace with herself and with the situation.

"I think it's because of the poem," she said later. "When I resigned myself to it and turned it all over to God, it just seemed to take part of the load off my shoulders."

Dr. Coster didn't come and ask for permission to turn off the machines that day. Tara seemed just the same to us, but the doctors said that her vital signs were growing stronger. She was putting up quite a fight.

It was now Friday, five days since Tara's admission to the hospital. It began to look as if this were going to be a long ordeal. I knew they needed me at the office, and I knew that

Donna needed me at the hospital with her, too. I also knew that my heart was with Donna and Tara. It was a tough decision, but I felt that unless things changed I should return to work on Monday.

Donna's mother, whom I call Tootie, had gone back on Thursday to her job as office manager of a large children's dental practice in Torrance, California. Our fathers, who are both business executives, had also found it necessary to return to work. Without my father to drive her on Southern California's famous freeways, my mother's visits were also curtailed.

The Hensons then sent for Donna's sister, Zane Christopher, to fly up from Houston, Texas, to keep her company. Zane is eleven years older than Donna, but looks much younger than her age, as all the Henson family do. Her dark hair, eyes, and complexion are in direct contrast to Donna's very light coloring. But they are very fond of one another, and I think we all felt relieved that Donna would have steady companionship.

We settled down to a rather routine existence. Donna and Zane traveled to the hospital early each day, while I went off to work. I often stopped by the hospital on my way to work and nearly always came by during my lunch hour. Then we spent all evening there and came home together. Often we were joined by our parents and other relatives and friends.

We became well acquainted with the doctors and nurses and other hospital personnel. We weren't thinking about more than one day at a time, but I guess we were beginning to think that things would go on like this forever. It seemed to us that our lives were suspended. Things progressed around us, but we stayed just the same.

Donna and I really missed Mark, but we didn't feel we were quite ready to have him come home. We didn't want things to be so disrupted when he came, and we didn't want to have to leave him with a baby-sitter all day. But we talked to him by phone each night, assuring him that we loved him and were anxious to have him with us.

One day, about two-and-one-half weeks after Tara's accident, we entered her room and were surprised to note that she was breathing on her own. The nurse said that the doctors were trying her without the respirator for short periods of time and that she seemed to be tolerating it well. We were so happy and thankful. Unable to really think up prayers on our own, we turned anxiously to our prayer book and began reading the portion dedicated to beginning recovery. Donna spent hours at Tara's bedside each day reading these prayers over and over, but still Tara lay in coma.

As time moved on, the doctors were able to leave the respirator off for longer and longer periods, until finally Tara reached the point where she was breathing on her own all the time. It seems like such a little thing—to breathe. After all, people do it every day and think nothing of it. We all take it for granted. But I don't think Donna and I will ever take breathing for granted again. Not after seeing Tara struggle and work for it minute by minute for more than two weeks. What a precious gift it is!

By now the doctors were beginning to say that Tara's very life was a miracle. She was growing stronger each day, although you certainly couldn't tell it by looking at her. She lay motionless, as always. Her eyes were still half-closed and unblinking, the pupils so enormous that her eyes looked black. She saw nothing, heard nothing, felt nothing. She didn't make the slightest sound and her face was completely expressionless.

At this point, the intravenous feedings were discontinued and a tube was put in her nose, down her throat, and into her stomach. This was to become Tara's lifeline to food for the next week. The catheterization continued because her bladder and kidneys still weren't functioning. We often tend to think that there is nothing as helpless as a newborn baby, but Tara was ever so much more helpless than that. We would have felt pleased had she been able to do even the things a newborn baby can do.

The doctors were happy, though, because she hadn't developed any of the secondary infections they had expected. They were standing by with medications for pneumonia and for the stomach and bladder disorders common in this type of patient, but they never had to use them.

It was August 23. Donna and I had spent the morning with Tara, talking to her, trying desperately to penetrate the coma that held her. Sitting there, looking at our once-beautiful baby, wondering if she would ever regain conciousness, was extremely discouraging. Donna and I had sunk into such a deep depression that even lunch at Farrell's ice cream parlor was unable to lift it.

Sadly we returned to put on our gowns and wash our hands. We slipped quietly to her bedside in the ICU, which had become her home. As we stood looking at her quiet, silent, unmoving face, I placed my fingers on her lips and started to recite a nursery rhyme she had always loved. As my fingers encircled her mouth I repeated:

> Bumble bee flies around the tree,
> Kazip, kazap,
> Kazee, zee, zee.

> Bumble bee flies around the tree,
> Kazip, kazap,
> Kazee, zee, zee.

And with that a light smile moved across her lips.

Our hearts jumped. We looked at each other and cried, "She smiled, she smiled!" The nurse looked up to see what the excitement was about. I said, "She smiled. Tara smiled!" The nurse, looking skeptical, hurried to Tara's bedside. To prove our point I placed my fingers on Tara's lips again and repeated:

> Bumble bee flies around the tree,
> Kazip, kazap.
> Kazee, zee, zee.

This time Tara did not smile. The nurse smiled at us, uttered a few encouraging words, and went back to her work. But we knew Tara had smiled. We rushed from the ICU and spread the good news to the family.

It was truly the beginning of Tara's recovery. From that point on, she started her slow emergence from coma into what is called stupor. From there she went to semiconsciousness and then to consciousness.

Just a few days before, a cardiac specialist had been called in to determine the significance of a heart murmur that had been observed. He decided this was not indicative of cardiac damage. However, just twenty-four hours after smiling, Tara expired without warning. Resuscitative measures were used and proved successful. They brought her back from her sixth heart stoppage since being admitted two weeks earlier.

From that day on Tara continued to get stronger, and decisions would soon have to be made as to what we were going to do with her. The hospital's and doctors' bills had skyrocketed into thousands of dollars by now, and we could not go on without a firm plan for her recuperation.

On August 26, the doctors transferred Tara to the special care unit on the first floor of the hospital. The move was made because they believed Tara was out of danger.

At this particular time Tara's eyes were open but she was totally blind, and only responded to our voices and to other noises around her.

One day that week, a nurse asked Donna if she wanted to hold Tara. With mixed feelings, Donna agreed. There was a deep yearning inside her to hold Tara once again, but this odd-looking child with the tube down her nose wasn't Tara at all. The experience was not only frightening but heart-breaking. Tara was as stiff as a board. Her legs didn't bend, her arms were rigid, and her head was thrown back in a stiff contraction. She shook all over and, though she was unable to speak, she wailed and moaned the entire time. Donna didn't feel as though she were holding a human baby at all.

A few days after her move to the first floor unit, I stopped by to see Tara on my way to pick up Mark in Woodland Hills, California, where he had been staying. I came through the double doors leading into special care, and proceeded to Tara's room. The nurse's station was vacant and the hallway deserted. As I looked up, I saw that the door to Tara's room was open.

My heart leaped with fear and a choking sensation filled my throat. Peering into her room, I noticed that it was so crowded with doctors and nurses that I was unable to see Tara lying on the bed. A doctor was leaning over Tara, his hand on her mouth. My mind raced. She's dying, she just can't make it back, was my anguished thought.

Hurriedly I moved closer, close enough to hear the conversation in the room. And there they were, sophisticated doctors and nurses, with years of training, and millions of dollars worth of medical equipment used to save lives and to detect when life and death are present. Instead, they were using the simplest of human gambits to gain recognition from a two-year-old, hurt bundle of humanity. That human trait of love. They all stood there as the doctor placed his fingers on her lips and repeated:

> Bumble bee flies around the tree,
> Kazip, kazap,
> Kazee, zee, zee.

I left the hospital and drove up the San Diego Freeway to the San Fernando Valley. As I wound my way through Woodland Hills to pick Mark up at my brother Tucker's home, I kept trying to think up answers to the questions I was sure my excited, vibrant five-year-old son was going to throw at me during our first reunion since Tara had been hurt nearly three weeks earlier.

The knock at the door brought my sister-in-law Nancy from her chores in the kitchen. She was full of questions. "How's Tara doing? When can she go home? How's Donna holding up?"

I answered each one as it came. Then my thoughts turned to Mark. "Where's Mark?"

"Out in the neighborhood with his cousins," Nancy replied.

I stood up and walked to the door, stepped out on the porch and gave a loud call for Mark. It didn't take long before Mark was bounding down the street in response to a familiar voice.

He shot across the lawn and threw his arms around my neck, holding me so tightly it felt like my neck was in a vise. Tears filled my eyes as he hugged me and told me how much he loved me and how he had missed his mother and me. His next rapid-fire questions were difficult.

"Daddy! Is Tara going to die? Will Tara ever be well again?"

I was honest with him. "No, we don't feel Tara will die," I told him. "She almost did, but she's better now. As to whether she will be well again, I just don't know, Mark."

We gathered up Mark's things and headed south toward Mission Viejo. It would be good to get Mark home and with his friends in the neighborhood again. Mark told me over and over again as we headed down the freeway how the fire department had come and administered oxygen to Tara. As only a five-year-old can do, he described the arrival of the ambulance and how Tara looked as though she were sleeping when they carried her from the house.

The events of the past weeks were rekindled as he described what his eyes had witnessed. My heart ached for Mark. I know now that this had been harder for him than I had imagined. I understood that Mark would need all the help and understanding we could give him in the months ahead to help him cope with the traumatic events taking place around him.

Donna met us as we drove into the driveway. She gathered Mark up in her arms and, as only a mother can do, expressed how pleased she was to have him home with her.

One evening (just for fun, as he put it), Dr. Ronar decided to feed Tara a popsicle. He didn't really expect that she would know what to do with one, and was shocked when she ate the entire thing. She seemed to enjoy it and we thought we could detect a sign of pleasure on her face. We wondered if she remembered the joy of eating good things.

They slowly withdrew the gastronasal tube over the next

two days, until Tara was taking all of her nourishment by mouth. She was so eager to eat that she reminded us of a newborn baby. She was fortunate in that she was able to eat table food cut into small pieces. We were told that people with injuries of this type normally can tolerate only strained baby food. Because of this, they don't get enough nourishment and become emaciated.

The daily ritual of going up to Children's Hospital was to continue for the next few weeks. During the waning days of August, a nurse broached to Donna the subject of our taking Tara home. Donna was petrified, and told me what the nurse had suggested.

"That's impossible," I replied, "Tara's in no condition to go home, and we're certainly not capable of caring for her." However, the talk of taking her home persisted over the next few days, and I was prompted to phone Dr. Ronar and ask him about it. Did he really think we should take Tara home? He said that this probably was a good time to consider it, and that he felt Tara would respond better in her own home, surrounded by familiar things.

By this time Mark was very anxious to see Tara, so we brought him to the hospital and let him look through the window at Tara lying in her bed. We had placed the bed by the window so he could get a glimpse of his baby sister, whom he had last seen being carried to an ambulance just weeks before.

Against our own judgment, we agreed to take Tara home. The next few days were spent in preparation for this big move. Nurses and therapists spent time with Donna showing her how to care for and to feed Tara.

The final procedures were outlined for the discharge, and the final cryptic notes in Tara's medical records stated:

At the time of discharge, Tara is unable to hold her head up, taking all feedings orally. She has spasticity of both upper and lower extremities. She hears and responds to oral stimuli, but is still blind.

5

Take Her Home and Love Her

Suddenly it was Saturday, September 3. The day dawned hot and clear, as is usual for Southern California in September. The Hensons had come down for the weekend and the entire household was up early. Mark was his normal hyperactive self, charging through the house and stirring things up in general.

It's funny how your entire perspective can change practically overnight. Mark had gone from the role of problem child to be worried over night and day, to that of a normal child, who would have to somehow fend for himself while we cared for the child who was desperately hurt.

The very air that day was charged with excitement. Tara was coming home! I think we all viewed the prospect with mixed emotions. What would it be like? How would it change our family? Forever the optimist, I welcomed the challenge. Maybe we could do something for Tara that the doctors couldn't. As for Donna, she was just plain scared. And for good reason. The burden of caring for Tara rested on her shoulders. I could go off to work every day, but Donna would be trapped in the house with this strange little person named Tara.

Donna began to cry that morning and just couldn't stop. We all tried to talk her out of it—her mother, her father, and I. Finally, we decided to leave her alone and let her cry herself out. She just couldn't stand the thought of bringing Tara home.

"She's not my daughter!" she screamed. "My beautiful little girl is dead! This little girl doesn't even look like her! It's bad enough that my baby is gone. If they gave me another sweet normal little two-year-old girl to have as my very own, it would still be hard. I would still miss Tara. But, instead, they are giving me a vegetable! And nobody understands why I'm not happy about it. Why? Why?"

She cried until at last there were no tears left, then washed her face and combed her hair. She had resigned herself to the situation. She squared her shoulders and determined to do the best job possible in the hope that one day Tara would be well again.

The Hensons had decided to take Mark through Lion Country Safari, a wild animal preserve, that day. You drove through it in your car and the animals just roamed wild all around you. Mark had never been there before and was excited about it. They would keep him out until we had arrived home with Tara and gotten ourselves organized. We wanted to keep life for Mark just as normal as possible.

We had arranged to meet with Dr. Ronar before we went to get Tara, hoping that he would have some specific instructions for us on how to care for her. Instead, we were to get our first clue that nobody really knew what to do with Tara.

"What exactly is wrong with Tara?" I asked the doctor. "Does it have a name?"

"When Tara suffered her skull fracture, she obviously received a violent blow on her head," he replied. "It was strong enough to cause her brain to bounce against her skull. This bruised her brain and also caused it to hemorrhage and swell, resulting in her coma. The swelling has gone down somewhat, so that she is partially conscious.

"The brain is the slowest organ in the body to heal. It will take some time for the bruises to go away and the blood to be reabsorbed into the bloodstream. As time goes on, the more the brain heals, the more Tara will be able to do. However, you must be prepared for the possibility that the brain may not heal at all. We'll just have to wait and see.

"Take her home and love her. Don't leave her in the crib all the time or she'll never improve. Stimulate her all you can. Turn on the radio for her if you leave her alone. Be sure to do her range of motion exercises two or three times a day and turn her and position her in bed so she won't get bedsores."

Thus armed, Donna and I strode into the hospital with as much confidence as we could muster. Although it had only been a month, it seemed almost as though we had spent all our lives at Children's Hospital. It felt odd to know that this would be our last day there, it had become so much a part of our lives.

"So this is the big day!" came greetings from nurses on the floor. "We're going to miss Tara. Bring her back so we can see how she is progressing. Good luck!"

Our hands trembled as we dressed Tara for her homecoming. Her arms and legs were as stiff as boards and she whined the spine-chilling cry that was to become so familiar to us in the weeks ahead. We remembered how frightened we had been when we had taken our first baby, Mark, home from the hospital. But that was nothing compared to the awesome task we now faced.

Tara was in her Easter dress now, the sunbonnet hiding her scarred little bald head. The stitch marks were still red and swollen, and the red family birthmarks also showed, since there was no hair to cover them. It was not a pretty sight, but under the bonnet you couldn't tell.

Since Tara could do absolutely nothing physically, a wheelchair was out of the question. They rolled her through the hospital on a bed. It was a triumphant procession, actually. A tiny girl had won her battle for life. Whatever the years ahead might bring, we knew that this small warrior deserved the best of everything we could offer. She deserved to get well! And we determined then and there to see to it that we neglected nothing in our effort to accomplish this goal.

I got behind the wheel of the car and the nurse handed Tara to Donna, who snuggled her close. Tara had gotten used to being held and didn't resist.

A trace of a smile crossed Tara's blank little face.

"She knows," we said.

And so we took our daughter home. Her eyes were wide open now, although the pupils were huge and she was still totally blind. They had a dull blank look and she didn't blink very often. The doctors weren't sure whether her sight would return when the retinal hemorrhages were absorbed into the bloodstream. They might leave scars on the eyes that would prevent vision. And there was the additional possibility that, even though the eyes themselves might return to normal, the visual center in the brain would be so damaged as to make sight impossible. We would just have to wait and see.

The facial muscles seemed slack, giving her face an unintelligent, expressionless look. Her mouth made funny little chewing motions almost all the time. She had gained a couple of pounds in the hospital, though; her face was filling out, and her cheeks had a rosy hue.

We knew Tara could hear, and felt that she also understood what she heard, because she smiled at the appropriate times. Some people said she had probably forgotten who she was or that she had even had a family. But we didn't think so. Donna and I maintained that she knew everything although, since she had so little in the way of responses, it was impossible to tell for sure.

Smiling seemed to be the only function Tara could perform voluntarily. Otherwise she was essentially unable to move. She had absolutely no head control, not even as much as a newborn baby. We had to be careful to cradle her head in our hands when we carried her or it would flop this way and that. The rest of her body was rigid and stiff.

Her arms had developed contractures. In her case this meant that they were bent at the elbow, while her tightly clenched little fists, with thumbs tucked inside, touched her shoulders. It was almost impossible to pry them open, and it took every ounce of strength I could muster to pull her arms out straight. As soon as I relaxed my hold, they would pop right back up again.

She kept her head thrust back and her back arched all the time. Her legs extended straight out, her toes pointed like a toe dancer's. She was unable to utter any sound, except for a shrill, tearless cry—something between a whine and a scream—that the doctors called a "brain cry."

This was the child we brought home. I pulled the car

into the driveway and turned off the ignition. The sun was hot as we carried Tara and her belongings into the air-conditioned house. Coco, our coca-poo puppy, met us at the door, jumping and barking excitedly.

"Tara, Coco's here. She's glad you're home," I said.

We carried Tara all through the house, stopping in each room and telling her where she was, reminding her of what she used to do there. It was only a guess on our part, but we sensed that she was happy to be home.

Some of our neighbors came over to see her. I think they were shocked by her condition, even though we had tried to prepare them for it. I guess the mind can't actually grasp such a state until confronted with it face to face. They had all known Tara since the day she was born and had grown to love this ever-smiling little girl. Now they were stunned, at a loss for words. Our family was suddenly avoided, something to talk about in hushed tones behind our backs.

It was in this atmosphere that we were to begin our new life. Our families were wonderful, coming down whenever they could. The first weekend after we got home with Tara, my brother Tucker and his wife Nancy came down to visit. They brought with them two books—*Run Away Little Girl* and *Todd*—that were to have a great impact on our life in the years ahead.

My parents and my sister Gale often came down for a day to lend a hand. In addition, a longtime family friend—Effie Kasperik—began at this time what has turned into a three-and-a-half-year pilgrimage. Driving the forty-mile distance from her home in Yorba Linda, each Wednesday she has come to help Donna with any household chores that need doing.

Donna's folks also provided tremendous assistance by spending nearly every weekend with us. They shopped for our groceries, cooked for us, and cleaned our house. They sent for the wonderful black woman, Lessie Cook, who had helped in their home in Houston from the time Donna was three years old until they moved to California when she was sixteen. Lessie came and spent two weeks with us right after Tara came home. She was a wonderful practical and emotional balm to Donna, caring for our family as if it were her own.

But even so, it was not easy. Tara didn't sleep well at night and often woke us up with her penetrating wail. Her mouth didn't work just right, so it took a long time to feed her. In addition, she drank just one sip at a time, nearly choking with each swallow, like a baby when it's being weaned to the cup. She was back in diapers.

And then there were the range of motion exercises. These, I know, bothered Donna more than anything else. They were difficult to administer, at best. Tara was so stiff that it took all of Donna's strength to perform them. Tara hated them and screamed all the way through them. By the time the exercises were completed, Donna would be physically and emotionally exhausted. She tried to do at least three hours of them a day, and I knew it was wearing her down.

Donna kept Tara in the room with her at all times, except for the two hours each afternoon when she napped. Tara was extremely unhappy a good deal of the time, and would lie on the floor and whine for hours on end. There was all this—plus the care of Mark, who was pretty demanding in his own right.

But there were bright spots, too. One day, about a week after we brought her home, Tara began to make little cooing sounds like a baby does. We didn't think much of it until our visit with Dr. Ronar. He was much impressed and said we could expect Tara to say a few words soon. He thought she looked much brighter and more alert than she had the last time he had examined her in the hospital. Donna and I were elated. Tara was making progress! We came home with a resolve to work even harder.

Sure enough, one night the following week, as we were sitting in the family room, Tara began to say "ma-ma-ma-ma." We were all so thrilled—Donna, Lessie, Mark, and I, that we were practically jumping up and down.

"Oh, Tara," we said, hugging her. "We're so proud of you."

"This baby's doing lots better," we overheard Lessie say to her daughter on the phone. "She can even say mama."

But the days were passing quickly, and soon Lessie's two weeks were up and she had to go back to Texas. We hated to have her leave; we really felt she had helped keep our family together.

Mark was starting back to school on Monday, and that meant Donna had to begin her sixty-mile round trip drive to Orange each day to take him to the special school he needed. We were trying to get Tara into a rehabilitation center in Orange, too, hoping to get times that coincided, so that Donna would only have to make one trip each day.

We had begun looking in earnest for a housekeeper, but were having very little luck. We could only afford to pay thirty dollars a week, and at that price there just weren't any to be found. We tried a woman from Mexico, but she only stayed one night and left without a word. Accordingly, for awhile we had no household help at all.

I often wonder how Donna managed to survive this period. I was gone a good deal of the time, even working some nights and weekends. It was very hard on her, especially the range-of-motion exercises. She began praying in earnest for some relief from this grueling task.

It was at this time that Eleanor Lau entered our lives. She just called one day, said she had heard about Tara, and offered to help. She told us she was a Christian, a born-again Christian, that she had been praying for a ministry, and thought that God wanted her to minister to Tara.

Donna and I had never heard anyone say anything quite like that before. I didn't put much stock in it, but I could see that Donna was greatly impressed.

"Don't you see?" she said. "God has answered my prayer. I know He has. No one I knew would help me, so He sent a stranger to us."

Eleanor came and was a great spiritual boon to Donna. She also organized some nine other Christian women to come and help with Tara's exercises. Each woman took an hour a week, and it was arranged so that there was someone there for an hour in the morning and an hour in the afternoon, Monday through Friday. That way Donna only had to spend one hour each day giving Tara her therapy.

Donna was amazed and kept telling me how wonderful these women were. "They don't even go to the same church," she marveled. "They're not doing it just because it's some women's club charity project. They're doing it because they want to. I've never known people like that before."

After three weeks, we were finally able to get Tara into the Easter Seal program. I know three weeks isn't very long, but we were so anxious to get professional help for Tara that it seemed like forever to us.

We took her in for evaluation on a Saturday. It was a very large rehabilitation center, housed in a big two-story building. There was a nice playground outside with lots of grass, a sandbox, and swings. Inside there was a large waiting room, with halls leading off in several directions, and an elevator to the second floor. The place was teeming with activity.

"Surely here they can help our Tara," we thought.

We were so excited, so hopeful. I guess we thought they could work miracles there overnight. They took her back and examined her. Donna and I were on needles and pins. We could hardly wait to hear their verdict. Finally they called us back down the long hall and into a small room furnished with a desk and some chairs.

"Tara has been severely injured, and has many problems," we were told. "We think it's best to concentrate on her physical disabilities. We'll schedule her for an hour a day, five days a week of therapy. She will receive half an hour of physical therapy and half an hour of occupational therapy."

"But I don't understand," Donna interrupted. "She's only two years old. She doesn't need to learn an occupation."

"Oh, no," the woman smiled. "By occupational therapy, we mean we will work with her on basic skills children should know, like playing with toys, things like that."

"But what about speech therapy?" I asked. "She's learned how to say mama and dada. Doesn't she need that, too?"

"Of course, it would be nice if Tara could learn how to talk," came the reply, "but right now her physical problems are so great, it's best to start there."

We were disappointed about the speech therapy, but were thrilled about their having accepted Tara.

"Now," we thought, "maybe with the proper therapy Tara will really start to improve." That was what we wanted more than anything.

We went over to a nearby ice cream parlor to celebrate. It was the first time we had taken Tara out in public since her accident, and she received more than a few strange looks.

"But you don't understand!" I wanted to yell. "She's really not like this at all! She's smart and pretty and smiles all the time!"

Instead I just gritted my teeth and said nothing. Donna was holding Tara in her arms, and Tara wore her usual blank look. The waitress was a young girl, who brought us our ice cream with a smile. She couldn't resist asking us about Tara and we explained it as best we could.

"I'm a volunteer over at Fairview State Hospital," she confided. "There are lots of children like Tara there."

Lots of children like Tara there, we thought. In a mental institution. But those children don't belong there. They should be with their families. Then maybe they could get well.

The following Monday brought yet another change of schedule for Donna. But this was to settle into a daily routine that would last for some time. We got up and got the children fed and dressed. Then I took Mark off to school on my way to work. One of the women came to give Tara her therapy for an hour, while Donna worked in the house. Then she and Tara drove to Easter Seal.

By the way, it's no simple matter to take a two-year-old child who can't sit up for a car ride. We put Tara in a car seat and just let her flop from side to side. It was distressing to watch, but it was about all we could do.

Tara spent an hour in therapy at Easter Seal, then it was back in the car and over to Providence Speech and Hearing Clinic to pick up Mark at school. It was a half-hour drive back home. Then Donna had to prepare lunch, feed Tara, and give her an hour of therapy. After that, Tara took a two-hour nap. When she woke up, another woman was there to give her another hour of therapy.

We were broadening her therapy, including procedures

54

the Easter Seal therapists had recommended. Her exercises now included an effort at sitting Indian style, rubbing and brushing her arms, pulling her arms out and holding them that way, tickling her, holding her upside down, and trying to get her to move. All this was done to the tune of children's records played on the living room stereo. By then, it was time for dinner, and the day began to wind down.

After a week or so of this routine, without any household help, Donna was beginning to get rather desperate. We felt that if we could only obtain full-time help for about six weeks, until Thanksgiving, Tara would be just that much better and Donna would be able to cope satisfactorily. Once more, she turned to prayer. A few days later, she got an unusual phone call. It was the voice of an older woman, asking if we needed a housekeeper.

"Why, yes," Donna said. "But how did you know?"

"The employment service gave me your number," came the reply.

"But I haven't contacted any employment service." By this time Donna was quite confused. "What number were you given?"

The number she read off wasn't our number at all. She had dialed incorrectly and gotten our number purely by chance. Donna could scarcely believe her ears.

"I've had two years experience," the voice went on, "and am out here visiting relatives. I would like to work only until Thanksgiving, when I will be going back to Michigan."

Realizing that she was a native American and that she sounded quite competent, Donna figured that she probably wanted far more money than we could afford to pay.

"How much do you charge?" she asked.

"Thirty dollars a week," came the reply.

They arranged for an interview that evening and Mrs. Crabb was hired on the spot. She was an elderly woman, the grandmother type, short and plump, with gray hair. She loved the children and was an excellent cook.

"If she's a Christian," Donna told me, "I'll know God answered my prayer."

The next night, Donna could hardly wait to tell me. "Mrs. Crabb is a Christian, a born-again Christian, just like Eleanor. I knew she would be. I knew that God had answered my prayer."

"What do you mean, born-again Christian?" I asked rather skeptically.

"I don't know," Donna said. "But it's a lot different from just going to church. These people really believe the Bible, and practice what it preaches. I think they're special."

Tara had been changing a little each day in the six weeks since we had brought her home from the hospital. They had been action-packed weeks but, unlike most busy times, they seemed to drag by. People were always asking us how Tara was doing. Donna's parents called every night to inquire.

Many times we felt sad, because we really didn't have anything concrete to tell them. She was changing, and over a period of six weeks she was a lot different. But the daily changes were so minor they were hardly noticeable.

When people were waiting for you to say that Tara was crawling, it seemed silly to say that her arms didn't seem to be bent up quite so much, or that she was pronouncing her mama and dada much more readily and with more meaning.

Every time Donna took her to see one of the consulting doctors, he would ask excitedly, "Is she standing up yet?" Donna could never understand how he expected a little girl who was just learning to hold up her head to be standing.

But there was no doubt in our minds that Tara was growing stronger and brighter each day. Her face was losing that blank stare and beginning to take on a look that seemed almost normal. She was smiling that special Tara smile again, and even laughed out loud sometimes. I would hold her in my arms and we would race through the house playing hide-and-seek with Mark. At times like these her laughter would echo through the rooms, mingled with Mark's and mine, just like it used to do. These were precious moments, to be treasured and remembered forever.

Her "brain cry" was gradually disappearing. We don't know exactly when it completely vanished. One day Donna and I just realized that it was gone. We were still worried about Tara's sight, though. The retinal hemorrhages had reabsorbed and miraculously left no scars on her eyes. But Tara was still blind. Her eyes were seeing, but the visual center in the brain was not picking up the images. Her speech wasn't coming along as we had hoped, either. It had been a month since she had first said mama, and she had added dada to it, but that was all.

I felt that Tara was a prisoner within her own body. Somewhere inside was the Tara we all knew and loved. Sometimes I just wanted to shout, "Let her out! Let my little girl out!"

Eleanor Lau had given Donna the book, *I Believe in Miracles,* by Kathryn Kuhlman. Miss Kuhlman believes she is a channel through which God heals people, and this book contains different case histories. Donna read it and was enthralled. She found out that Kathryn Kuhlman came to the Shrine Auditorium in Los Angeles once a month, and asked me if she could take Tara. I told her she could, but that I wouldn't go with her.

Through Eleanor, Donna met Harry and Donna Edwards, a couple who live in the neighboring town of El Toro. Mr. Edwards is an usher for Kathryn Kuhlman at the Shrine Auditorium, and they were kind enough to take Donna and Tara to Los Angeles to see her. It was a long day for them. They left home early that Sunday morning and didn't return until after seven that night. They both looked exhausted.

We fed Tara a quick dinner and put her to bed. After we had tucked Mark in, Donna and I had a chance to talk.

"What was it like?" I asked.

"I've never seen anything like it before," Donna said. "I don't think you would like it, but I could certainly feel God's presence there."

"Did any people get healed?" was my next question.

"Well," Donna replied, "people went up and said they had been healed." Then she shrugged sadly. "I sure wish Tara had gotten healed today. She did say another word though. She said 'bye-bye' as we were leaving the auditorium." Then she looked at me rather shyly. "Mike, I became a Christian today. They had an altar call and I went up and gave my life to Jesus."

I really didn't know what to make of that, so I just turned out the light and said good night.

The ensuing weeks were really exciting ones for us. The very next day Tara began learning about eight new words a day. Donna and I were ecstatic. Even the doctors were pleased.

Halloween was coming up, and there really wasn't any

question in our minds that Tara would go trick-or-treating. Mark and Tara would both be tigers. Donna made a long tail for Tara and tied a ribbon at the end of it.

It was cold and crisp on the big night. Donna and I were secretly worried. "What would the neighbors think?"

We dressed the children carefully, and painted whiskers on their faces. Tara had a wig to cover her little bald head and Donna had put an orange ribbon in it. Wigs are not made for a two-year-old, so this one was slightly large. It slipped all around on Tara's head, and we were constantly having to straighten it. She couldn't begin to sit up, so we took turns carrying her from house to house.

The night was filled with laughing children of all ages, darting here and there. As we carried our daughter that night, holding out her jack-o'-lantern for her while Mark said trick-or-treat, we were once more brought face-to-face with the severity of Tara's handicap. She was so different from the costumed children that she might have been a visitor from another planet. It was so hard to understand and even harder to accept.

The days slipped by, and soon it was Thanksgiving. My family was having a reunion at my sister's house in Las Vegas. As I look back on it, I can't imagine that I would leave Donna for a major holiday at a time like that, but that's exactly what I did. I know it must have been extremely difficult for her, but she didn't complain.

In a way, it was a nice change of pace for her. She and the children went to stay with her parents in Palos Verdes for the weekend. When I returned home Saturday evening, I found that Mark was ill. He was vomiting, his head hurt, and he was running a high temperature. A local doctor had diagnosed it as tonsillitis and had him on antibiotics.

But Mark kept getting worse, and by Monday morning Donna and I were really concerned. I took him to our pediatrician, who said he thought Mark had spinal meningitis. My heart just sank. I had seen meningitis cases at the hospital while Tara had been there, and realized it was often fatal and sometimes left brain damage. As they were taking the spinal tap on Mark to confirm their suspicions, I just sat there in a virtual stupor. It didn't seem possible that tragedy could strike again so soon.

"It is the aseptic viral strain of meningitis," the doctor ultimately explained. "Not nearly as dangerous as the bacterial variety and never fatal. It normally doesn't leave any aftereffects either."

I gave a long sigh of relief.

"Since a virus is causing it," he continued, "we can't treat it with antibiotics. It will just have to run its course. I'll give Mark suppositories for the headaches and the vomiting."

He was quiet for a moment, then added, "Maybe it would be best if you didn't tell Donna. She has enough to worry about. Just tell her he has a bad case of the flu."

I know I was shaking as I drove Mark home. He was so sick—sicker than I'd ever seen him. His cheeks were pale and there were dark circles under his eyes. It seemed to take all his strength just to sit up in the car, and he didn't have the energy to talk. I wondered what I would tell Donna. Should I tell her the truth? Should I follow the doctor's advice?

I finally decided on the latter, girded myself with as much strength as I could muster, and strode into the house. Donna was already concerned because we had been gone so long.

"Mark is too sick to be kept out like this," she said. "How could they have made you wait?"

"They took a spinal tap." I said carefully. She took a deep breath. "They thought Mark might have spinal meningitis, but it turned out that he didn't. Just a strong strain of virus." I couldn't look her straight in the eye and tell such a blatant lie, but she was so relieved she didn't suspect I was not telling the truth.

"Is he contagious?" she asked.

"I don't know, but I'd sure keep him away from Tara as much as possible."

I had already booked myself heavily with evening appointments that week and would come in around ten each night to find Donna exhausted from caring for the two children.

Mark had been vomiting now for five days and had barely been able to keep anything down. Wednesday night Donna seemed especially upset.

"He's so sick," she said. "He just isn't getting any better. He hasn't even been able to urinate for two days. I got him to keep down half a popsicle today, but he just lost it."

Just then, a weak cry came from Mark's bedroom. "Is that Mark?" I asked, shocked at his pathetic tone.

"Yes," Donna said, as we rushed to his room.

He was vomiting again and it was black. He was so weak he could barely lift his head off the pillow and his eyes were sunk into his head and were only partially open. He had lost so much weight he could have passed for a refugee from a concentration camp. His voice was so weak we could barely understand him.

"Mike," Donna said, "please call the doctor. I'm so worried. I think he's dehydrated. You know you can go into a coma from that and even die from it."

As is usually the case when you need a physician, ours was not available and had not alerted the doctor on call about

Mark's case. I tried to get Donna to leave the room, but she was glued to the spot waiting anxiously to see what the doctor would say.

There was no other way—I had to tell him Mark had spinal meningitis and then described his current condition. To my surprise, he was most unsympathetic and told us to give Mark another suppository for the vomiting. That was all.

I hated to face Donna, but she was much calmer about my deception than I thought she would be.

"I don't care what you want to call it," she said. "Mark is very ill and I have known that all along."

We gave Mark the suppository, but an hour later he was vomiting again. Again we called the doctor, but he was equally unresponsive. Donna called Children's Hospital to see if they would check Mark for us if we brought him in, but they said no, not without doctor's orders.

It was really late now—nearly midnight. Donna and I went to bed, but couldn't sleep. Donna was afraid Mark would be in a coma before the night was out. Indeed, I admitted to myself that he looked awfully close to it already. He vomited once more around two in the morning and seemed worse to us than he had before.

Again I called the doctor. This time he was really angry and downright rude. As a matter of fact, he hung up on me. Donna and I felt completely helpless. We had no one to turn to, our son was dangerously ill, and nobody would listen to us.

As a last resort, Donna began to pray. Within fifteen minutes, the doctor called us back and said that he had reserved a room for Mark at Children's Hospital and that they were expecting us. We were so thankful. We called a neighbor over to stay with Tara and piled ourselves into the car.

The resident on duty at the hospital confirmed our fears. Mark was dehydrated and was put in the special care unit on intravenous feeding immediately. We stayed for awhile, and when we were certain things were under control we left for home. At four in the morning, we fell into bed for a restless three hours' sleep before the new day would begin.

6

In Search of Help

Tara woke up around seven that morning and Donna and I dragged ourselves out of bed to begin the day's activities. I reached for the phone on the bedside table and called Children's Hospital to find out how Mark was doing. The nurse reported that he was asleep and was doing better than he had been upon admittance.

Donna then headed for Tara's room because she had to be fed, bathed, dressed, and made ready for the morning helper to put her through her exercise routine. I hurried off to work and Donna began her preparations for taking Tara to Easter Seal for therapy.

While Tara was in therapy, Donna rushed over to the hospital to see Mark, who looked somewhat better after several hours of intravenous feeding. It was a relief to know that he was in good hands and was going to be all right.

I took that afternoon and the next day off from work so I could be with Mark. He was behaving much better than I had thought he would with the intravenous needle in his arm, and I was proud of him. The poor little guy had gone through quite an ordeal these past few months, but he seemed to be taking things in his stride. Our pediatrician was surprised and pleased to see how well Mark was accepting the changes that had taken place in our household.

After two days of hospital care, Mark was well enough to come home. The nurses in special care had remembered Tara and had asked us to bring her in for a visit, so we took her with us when we went to pick up Mark.

The hospital staff was pleasantly surprised to see the progress Tara was making. She smiled and told them "hi." We proudly showed off her greatest accomplishment, which was her ability to name the parts of her body. We pointed to the different parts such as eyes, lips, nose, arms, legs, and stomach, and she told us correctly what they were. She held her little head just as straight as she could and her unseeing eyes twinkled from under her wig. Mark was well on the road to recovery, and Donna and I felt things were certainly looking up.

On the following Tuesday, Tara grew quite listless and began running a temperature. Donna took her in to Dr. Ronar, who was immediately concerned and said that Tara had contracted Mark's virus.

"Don't worry," he said, "it's not meningitis. It has settled in her chest and throat. But make no mistake, she's a sick little girl, and she'll get worse before she gets better. She'll probably run a high temperature with this. Antibiotics won't touch the virus, but I'm going to give her some anyway in hopes of warding off complications."

"Could the virus spread to her spine and become meningitis?" Donna asked.

Dr. Ronar was silent for a moment and then admitted that it could.

Mark still hadn't gone back to school, so Donna sadly drove home with the two children. The doctor was right; Tara did get worse. She was still so weak, and her temperature stayed around 105°. She was on Dilantin and Valium, which are anticonvulsants, prescribed to offset the seizures she had suffered in the hospital.

Donna was terrified that the high fever would bring on more convulsions. She spent most of her time rocking Tara, singing to her, and trying every way she knew to bring her temperature down. She had spent nearly three weeks now giving tepid baths and alcohol rubdowns first to Mark and now to Tara. Tara's bright little smile was fading once more and she whined and cried incessantly.

Friday morning Tara seemed much worse and began to vomit. Donna got everything done and was ready to take her in to the doctors as soon as they opened. But when she called, the nurse said she would have Dr. Ronar call her back.

Donna was fit to be tied when nine-thirty and then ten came and went and still the doctor hadn't called. She phoned me at work to say Tara had vomited two more times and was extremely ill. She had been unable to keep down her anticonvulsant drugs. What if she had a seizure?

Donna waited endlessly that long morning, and watched as Tara became sicker and sicker. She called the doctor's office back again at eleven, but still received no help. Finally, at noon, Dr. Ronar phoned. He hold her he was on his way to lunch and would see Tara at two-thirty.

Meanwhile, Donna sat by Tara's crib and watched her

little girl wilt like a flower without water. I drove home and found Donna at Tara's bedside, deep in prayer. I was shocked to see the condition Tara was in. My mind flashed back to painful memories of Tara in coma, and I realized that she now looked almost the same. She was just lying there, still and quiet. Her eyes were half-closed and unblinking, her breathing shallow and labored. Her little body felt as if it were on fire.

"Tara, Tara," I cried, "are you all right?"

"Yes, Daddy," she whispered. Her voice was normally weak, but now I could scarcely hear her at all. Tears stung my eyes as I gathered her up and carried her to the car.

Dr. Ronar took one look at her and told us to take her straight to Children's Hospital. The resident doctor on the third floor informed us that Tara was badly dehydrated and must be put on intravenous feeding immediately. They shooed Donna and me from the room and began the procedure. Donna and I waited in the hallway, listening to Tara's weak whimper. We couldn't understand why it was taking so long and, as the minutes dragged by, we began pacing up and down worriedly.

Finally, a team of strained and weary people appeared from Tara's room to say that her veins were collapsed because of all the intravenous work performed on her in August. It had taken them an hour and a half, trying first one place and then another, before they ultimately found a vein that would take the needle. They had carefully attached it to Tara's foot.

"Oh, my sweet little Tara," I thought. "Why must everything be so hard for you?"

She was put in isolation, because they weren't sure whether or not she had spinal meningitis. Dr. Ronar came in later to examine her. He said she had viral syndrome. Her body was still so weak from the trauma of her injury in August, that the virus had spread all over her system. Her tonsils, eyes, ears, nose, chest, and stomach were infected.

"What about her spine?" I inquired anxiously.

"I don't know," he replied. "We'd have to take a spinal tap to find out. Frankly, I think she's too ill to tolerate one. It doesn't matter anyway. We'll treat it the same way regardless."

That afternoon I was in the hallway outside Tara's room when Dr. Coster, the surgeon who had performed Tara's operation back in August, walked down the hall. He looked quite surprised to see me. He inquired about Tara, and I informed him that she was inside the room suffering from a massive infection in her body. Concerned, he put on a gown and went to her bedside. He emerged a few minutes later and tried to encourage me with a few kind words. He was so proud of Tara because, as he said, "a brain surgeon doesn't have many successes."

The next day they put a little two-year-old boy in the room with Tara. His name was Andy, and he had curly red hair. He had swallowed some pills and was in for observation. It was nerve-racking to spend two days in a small hospital room with a normal two-year-old. He was up and down and running around, full of talk and activity. The comparison to Tara was simply overwhelming. Had she really been so full of life just four months ago? It seemed hard to believe. It was difficult to remember just how Tara used to be. Fortunately, by Sunday afternoon Tara's condition had improved so much that we were able to take her home.

It was December 13 now, and Christmas was fast approaching. Donna had made friends with some of the other mothers of children taking treatment at Easter Seal, and they were going Christmas shopping while the children were in therapy. It had been difficult for Donna to adjust to Easter Seal. The very name, Easter Seal Rehabilitation Center for Crippled Children and Adults, was upsetting to her. She hated to think of Tara as crippled. She just couldn't bring herself to accept the fact that Tara really was like the other children there.

I remember one day shortly after Tara started her treatment there, the other mothers were explaining to Donna what was wrong with their children. Many of them had cerebral palsy. This was a term we had heard, but we were uncertain as to what it meant. We had previously thought it was some kind of disease.

They explained that it was the name given to any kind of muscle impairment due to brain damage. Donna had rushed home and phoned me at work, insisting that I call the doctor and ask him if Tara had cerebral palsy.

I took Dr. Ronar by surprise with my inquiry, and he didn't really want to answer me. He finally admitted that cerebral palsy was a garbage-dump phrase that included, sooner or later, nearly every kind of brain damage. He said he didn't want to pin that label on Tara.

This was still another in a long line of upsets for Donna and me. We still hated to even mention the word brain damage out loud, and preferred just to say that Tara had had an accident. Somehow, it sounded better. And now to realize she actually had cerebral palsy—that really sounded horrible!

Actually, the other patients at Easter Seal were better than Tara in many ways. And, as the weeks went by, Donna began to realize this. She started to look past the handicap and into the individual child involved in each case. She grew increasingly fond of these little people, each one struggling for his own identity and place in the normal world. Donna began to realize how much she had in common with the other young mothers, as they sat and discussed the joys and failures they had experienced with their special children.

She became especially fond of Bobbie Merritt, the pretty blond mother of two-year-old Christie. Christie had been brain-injured at birth and had cerebral palsy. She was a beautiful child, with long honey-colored curls, bright blue eyes, and dimples. She could creep on her hands and knees, use her right hand and do lots of things that Tara couldn't do. Partly because she had the same sweet disposition as Tara, the two became friends.

One day, just before Christmas, as the therapist carried Tara out to Donna, Tara said, "I see Mommy."

Donna told me she didn't think there was a dry eye in the room that day. For some time, we had felt that Tara's vision was improving. But it was hard to tell just how much she could see. How wonderful to know that she could see well enough to pick her mother out of a group of women.

They were giving Tara ice-water treatments in an effort to reduce the spasticity in her muscles. For five minutes each day, they would lower Tara into a tank of 45° water. When they brought her out to Donna, she would be nearly blue and shaking violently all over, her teeth chattering.

"No like ice," she would say in her most convincing voice.

She spoke mostly in a soft monotone, but the ice-water treatment usually inspired her to use a little more expression.

Donna and I experienced mixed emotions that Christmas day. I think it is always a difficult time for people to endure shortly after a tragedy. We thought back to the Christmas we had celebrated the year before and to how Tara at a year and a half had loved it. We remembered her look of amazement as she had walked in and beheld the splendor of the decorated, lighted tree and the gifts that morning. This year, as I carried her to the family room, I wondered to myself if Tara would ever be able to walk again. However, we were tremendously thankful that Tara was still alive; we thought of her as our very own special Christmas angel. We were immensely proud of her accomplishments and her tremendous desire to do things.

"I will walk," she would say, with all the conviction that a two-and-one-half-year-old can muster.

Tara's dark hair had finally grown enough to cover her head. It's growth had been sporadic. In fact, around the incisions it hadn't grown at all for a long while. We had been afraid that perhaps it would never come in right, and were thrilled that by Christmas she had a very short little pixie hairstyle and could go without her wig. I know this really meant a lot to Donna.

Donna's sister Marilyn had come out from Texas to spend Christmas with her family. For some time we had looked forward to visiting with her and her two children. We drove up to the Henson home in Palos Verdes and planned to spend the day after Christmas there. Marilyn is nine years older than Donna—very young looking and attractive, with light-brown hair and blue eyes. She had with her twelve-year-old Joel and two-and-a-half-year-old Elizabeth. Elizabeth was two months older than Tara, a pretty little girl with long blond curls and huge brown eyes. The last time we had seen her, she and Tara had each been a year old and had been neck and neck in speech and development.

To see Elizabeth running and playing was almost too much to bear. Her squeals of laughter rang through the house as she and Mark rushed here and there, playing with the Christmas toys. We had forgotten how much fun Mark and Tara used to have playing together. This day really brought back memories of how Tara used to be and of how she would be now had she not been injured. I think it must have made even Tara sad because she was unusually quiet and withdrawn all day. On the way home that night, Mark was full of talk about Elizabeth and all the fun they had had together.

"Tara isn't any fun," he said. "Why did she have to get hurt so we can't play together? It's not fair—I want a sister like Elizabeth."

"No," I thought. "It certainly isn't fair. But then, nobody ever said life was going to be fair."

The next day was the worst one Donna had ever experienced. She and I had adjusted to Tara quite well, I thought. We were really doing nicely. But spending the day with Elizabeth proved to be too much for Donna. She was in hysterics all that day. Nothing I did stemmed the flow of her tears, or helped lighten the crushing sense of depression that gripped her. In desperation, I called her parents and they drove down right away. But even they had no effect on her mood. We were really frightened. What if Donna were having a nervous breakdown? What would happen to us? Toward evening Donna finally cried herself out, and the next day she was fine.

After the episode with Elizabeth, Donna and I were more determined than ever that Tara should one day be well. She had begun her life in the perfection that God had intended for her. And then she had been robbed. She had had her perfection taken away from her. God, we felt, had meant that she should be able to run and to play and to do all the things little girls can do. Accordingly we would stop at nothing to see that someday she would, in fact, do those things. We determined not to accept defeat.

The following Sunday, Harry and Donna Edwards, the couple who had taken Donna to see Kathryn Kuhlman, once again invited us to attend church with them. They were members of Melodyland Christian Center, a large non-denominational church in Anaheim, located across the street from Disneyland. Donna had gone with them several times, but I had always declined. This time I agreed to go along.

We put Mark in a Sunday school class, but Tara had to come into church with us because only we knew what to do with her. She was restless and irritable, so I spent most of the service holding her and walking back and forth at the rear of the building.

Having been raised in the formal rituals of the Episcopal church, I felt ill at ease there and really didn't get much out of the service. Therefore, I was immensely surprised when I felt my hand going into the air at the close of the program when the pastor asked people to accept Jesus as their personal Lord and Savior.

Before I realized it, I found myself in the aisle, making my way toward the altar with hundreds of other people. There I was, repeating the sinner's prayer and asking Jesus to come into my heart and into my life.

What an experience! I can say with conviction that I have never been the same since. My life has been immeasurably changed for the better. Donna was so thankful that she could share her Christian life with me, and the character and flavor of our home and our marriage changed as we started to grow together as Christians.

Meanwhile, Tara was continuing to change. Day by day, we watched a beautiful butterfly emerge from her cocoon of brain damage. And the lovely child she was becoming was a true joy to us all. Mark could talk to her now—tease her and make her squeal. In the way of children, he accepted her and treated her just as all brothers must treat their younger sisters, with that curious mixture of love and contempt.

Nevertheless, as spring approached, Tara was still virtually without movement. We waited in vain for her to begin to do something. She was sweet and pretty and smart. We had been able to stop worrying about the possibility that she might be mentally retarded. This had previously been our greatest fear, but the fear of handling a lifelong cripple now loomed ahead of us.

It's funny, but people usually think of a cripple as someone who is unable to walk, someone who is confined to a wheelchair or perhaps needs the assistance of leg braces or crutches in order to get around. I've even heard of people who walk with a limp referred to as crippled. It was difficult for people to realize that here was a little girl who had extreme difficulty performing the simple task of holding up her head, and that this was the only real activity that she could perform at all. Sit up in a wheelchair? She couldn't sit up anywhere!

Tara had a stroller that Donna occasionally used to take her for walks. The sight of the two of them would have been funny had it not been so terribly sad. We live in the hills, and the sidewalks are full of curves and marked by steep inclines. Tara would try valiantly to maintain her sitting balance, but it was just impossible. She would flop forward and backward, to the right and to the left, depending upon the direction of the sidewalk. Every few steps, Donna would be forced to stop and prop her up.

It grew increasingly difficult to take her places. She was nearing three years of age and weighed twenty-nine pounds. Hers was a dead weight because she couldn't support herself, nor could she help herself by holding onto any object. We grew more and more weary of the comments we received each time we took Tara out in public.

74

It was always either, "My, she must be getting heavy," or "Oh, you have a sleepy one today." And there were the ever-present questions from well-meaning friends. "How is Tara doing?"—"Oh, fine," we would say. How could we ever explain to them? Our own feelings and reactions were so complicated and so difficult to put into words.

It was at this time that we were working with a group of parents in an effort to bring special education classes to our local schools. Many of us felt that sixty miles and more was just too far to have to take our youngsters for schooling. At one of the school board meetings, Donna and I had the opportunity to meet Corinne Parker, one of the leaders of the group.

She was a dynamic, positive woman, the mother of three children. Her youngest, Michael, had been brain-damaged at birth. It had taken him until he was two years old to learn to hold up his head, but he was four now and could walk and run perfectly. Here was the subject dearest to our hearts.

Donna went down to meet Michael a few days later and was extremely impressed.

"He really can walk and run," she said. "To look at him, you'd never know he had cerebral palsy. But he can't speak. They're working very hard on that problem right now."

"What is their secret?" I wanted to know.

"A lot of hard work, and faith in God." Donna replied. "They took Michael to UCLA for his physical therapy. Maybe we should take Tara there."

Accordingly, we called and made an appointment at the UCLA Cerebral Palsy Clinic. They X-rayed and evaluated Tara thoroughly and told us that she was extremely spastic. In fact, her legs scissored worse than any they had ever seen.

"Do you think she can learn to walk?" we asked.

"I don't know," came the reply from one of the examining physicians. "It will take many years and she will never walk normally. She may never learn at all."

"But what about Michael Parker?" Donna wanted to know. "You said he would never be able to do anything, either."

"We really can't explain it," the doctor admitted. "Sometimes these children do much better than we expect them to; at other times they don't."

Donna and I left UCLA that day more determined than ever to bring about Tara's complete recovery. We looked over at our beautiful, intelligent daughter. We thought of her patient, sweet disposition. We thought of the future: of sixteen-year-old Tara who would want boyfriends and dates; of twenty-one-year-old Tara who would want a husband and children. Our wonderful daughter not walk? No, we just couldn't accept that. There must be another way. We would just have to keep searching.

Bobbie and Steve Merritt, the parents of Tara's friend, Christie, were going through a similar crisis. Christie was pulling her body up to stand, and the therapists at Easter Seal were talking about crutches for her. That is, some time in the future when her left hand had improved enough to be able to hold them. The orthopedic doctor put braces on her legs, which he said she must wear indefinitely. Then he warned that she might need surgery in her legs to help her walk.

Like us, this was not what the Merritts wanted for their beautiful, intelligent daughter. They, too, determined to stop at nothing to see that Christie could walk, and walk perfectly—that she could use her left arm and hand as well as her right.

Apparently, this was Donna's and Bobbie's main topic of

conversation while their girls were receiving therapy at Easter Seal. There must be a way, and these two determined young mothers were going to find it!

Bobbie had another friend whose little boy, Curt, had incurred severe brain damage. Like Christie, the umbilical cord had strangled him at birth and cut off the oxygen supply to his brain. But his brain had been more seriously damaged than Christie's. The administrators at Easter Seal wouldn't accept him as a patient because they felt he couldn't be helped. Doctors had advised his young parents to institutionalize him, that he was hopelessly physically and mentally retarded.

Gil and Melinda Stroschein decided to try other avenues anyway. They had heard of a place in Philadelphia called the Institutes for the Achievement of Human Potential, the largest brain institute for children in the world. They understood that it would accept anyone for treatment, regardless of the severity of brain damage, and that they had had some success with children as badly injured and incapacitated as Curt. They were currently waiting for their appointment in Philadelphia, which was in April.

Donna and Bobbie were anxious to see how the visit would go. Maybe here was the place to help their girls. Steve and I were unimpressed. However, Donna asked me to read a book about a little girl not unlike Tara. It was called *Run Away Little Girl.*

The story dealt with a family's determination to bring their daughter out of the world of brain damage. It told of this place in Philadelphia, and how the doctors and therapists there were achieving success with hurt kids like Tara and Christie. We learned, however, that the local doctors were totally against the Institutes and their unconventional approach to brain damage.

When the Stroscheins returned from their weeklong visit to Philadelphia, Bobbie was one of the first ones over to see if she could help in Curt's extensive recuperative program. She was quickly caught up in Melinda's enthusiasm and persuaded Donna to come along to see what Curt was doing.

That evening, Donna could hardly wait for me to come home from work. "I've found it! I've found it!" she cried. "I've found the place to help Tara!"

I dared not let hope rise up inside me. "What do you mean?" I asked.

"I went to see Curt today. You should see what they're doing with him. It's really exciting! Won't you go see?"

Reluctantly, I agreed. The next day, Donna and I visited the Stroscheins together. You could feel the excitement in the house when Melinda Stroschein, a vivacious, pretty woman with long dark hair and flashing dark eyes, met us at the door and drew us inside. In the middle of her living room perched a large wooden slide, and lying on the slide was a little blond-haired boy.

"This is Curt," Melinda bubbled. "He's learning how to crawl. He can move himself all the way down this slide with gravity to help him. Before this, he could never move at all."

She showed us his various pieces of equipment and told us all about his eight-hour-a-day therapy program.

I felt encouraged but skeptical. It certainly looked like a good program. They were doing much more with Curt than anyone had told us to do for Tara. But I was still concerned because so many doctors were against the procedure. Donna, however, was sold on the idea, and so was her friend Bobbie. I think the two of them must have spent hours dreaming up ways to convince their husbands that here was the place for which they had been searching.

Donna and I were both doing a great deal of praying,

asking God to show us what he wanted us to do for Tara. She had come to a standstill at Easter Seal, and finally the therapist there told Donna that they would be cutting Tara's therapy time in half to make room for someone who might progress better than Tara on their program. Donna and I were crushed. Surely if Tara weren't progressing, what she needed was more therapy, not less.

On our next visit to UCLA, we asked the doctor in charge there what she thought about the Institutes for the Achievement of Human Potential in Philadelphia. She obviously didn't approve although, like the others we had asked, she didn't really have any concrete reason as to why she didn't.

"Of course," she said disdainfully, "almost anybody would improve on eight hours of therapy a day.".

"Good grief," Donna said to me as we walked toward the parking lot. "If Tara would improve on eight hours a day of therapy, why doesn't somebody give us an eight-hour-a-day therapy program?"

She finally persuaded me to let her write to Philadelphia for an appointment. "If you decide against it when the time comes, we can always cancel it."

So we finally made our decision, and were sent an appointment date of September 13, 1971. Tara's friend Christie was sent an appointment for October, so the little girls would begin around the same time.

Tara now had twenty women assisting with her therapy regime at home. Donna had grown quite fond of them, and they had been a great help to her over the past several months. She began to tell them of the exciting new plan we had for Tara, and her enthusiasm was catching. Margo Clarke, an attractive young mother of three, volunteered to help Donna acquire and coordinate the many people it would take to put Tara through her patterning program.

One day when Donna took Mark and Tara to the pediatrician for their checkups, she gathered up her courage to tell him of our decision to bring Tara to the Institutes. He was very displeased and told Donna that we were wasting our time trying to help Tara.

"Spend your time on the child who has the greatest potential," he said.

"I believe that both my children have good potential," Donna retorted, "and I intend to spend as much time as necessary on each of them to see that they are able to achieve their highest potential."

I'll never understand why doctors speak as they do in front of children. Every time one would begin talking about Tara and her problems, it would be so upsetting to her that she would just hang her head.

Meanwhile, the weeks were speeding by, and the day of our departure for the East Coast was fast approaching. We had decided to take the whole family—Donna, Mark, Tara, and myself—and enjoy a three-week vacation first. My brother Tucker, his wife Nancy, and their three daughters had moved to Summit, New Jersey, during the year and we decided to make their home our headquarters.

When the big day finally arrived, our excitement was tempered with sadness. Donna's parents were moving back to Texas. They would be gone by the time we returned from our trip East, and we knew their absence would leave a special gap in our lives that no one else could ever fill. So it was that we boarded the jet plane with smiles on our faces and tears in our eyes.

7

Congratulations, Your Daughter
Is Brain-Injured

A five-hour plane flight with two small children can be quite an experience, and this was certainly so in our case. Tara had become carsick on the way to the airport, so she and Donna, who had been holding her on her lap, both smelled like sour milk for the duration of the flight. And Mark was always a problem to us when traveling. Because he was hyperactive, he found it virtually impossible to sit still and be quiet for long periods of time. He and the stewardesses took turns locking each other in the galley, and they finally let him hand out the junior pilot wings to all the children on board. He even got to go into the cockpit with the pilots after we landed.

Tucker and Nancy were there waiting for us in the congested Newark, New Jersey, airport. Tara now had a little umbrella stroller that tilted backward, so she didn't have to work as hard at sitting up. However, she still flopped from side to side, and I'm sure Tucker and Nancy were somewhat disappointed to see how little physical progress Tara had made in the past eight months since they had last seen her. I don't think any of us had yet realized how very slow progress comes to children like Tara.

We had decided to suspend Tara's therapy for three weeks and really enjoy our vacation. What a thrill it was to visit so many of our historic American cities. It had been years since I had been on the East Coast, and Donna had never been further east than Arkansas. The children were too young to really comprehend the importance of the places we visited, but that didn't keep them from enjoying themselves. For three glorious weeks we were more carefree than we had been in a long time.

We went to New York City, and then into Uncasville, Connecticut, where we met our future sister-in-law, Chris, who was to marry Donna's younger brother, Doug, in October. We saw the lovely old homes of Newport, Rhode Island, and the picturesque beaches of Cape Cod, Massachusetts. Donna fell in love with Boston, which was her favorite of the cities we visited.

The children enjoyed the hurricane that hit Boston while we were there. Being native Californians, they had never witnessed anything quite like it before. Tara and Mark loved building sand castles and digging for clams at Bay Head on the Jersey shore. But I think I enjoyed Washington, D.C. the most. It was truly awe-inspiring to stand before such historic buildings as the White House. And, of course, Mount Vernon and the placid Potomac River enthralled us all.

The carefree days passed quickly, however, and soon it was time to kiss Mark good-bye and head for Philadelphia with Tara. Tucker and Nancy were kind enough to watch Mark for us while we spent the week at the Institutes.

We drove the 150 miles to Philadelphia on Sunday, September 12, in a blinding rainstorm. But even that rain couldn't dampen our spirits that day. We were proud of Tara and hopeful that the Institutes could help her. She had truly enjoyed our vacation and was just sparkling from it. Her voice seemed stronger and she was putting more expression into it.

That Monday morning, at our hotel, we were up bright and early, our excitement so great you could feel it in the air. For once, even Donna was on time, and we pulled into the driveway at the Institutes precisely at nine.

I don't know what we had expected—something like a hospital, I suppose. But we soon discovered that the Institutes was situated on the grounds of what was once a large elegant estate. It had beautifully manicured lawns and large old trees, with several buildings, both old and new, scattered about.

We were directed to a rather small one-story, houselike structure that contained the reception and evaluation rooms. Opening the door, we found ourselves in a very large room, bare of any furniture save a clothes rack at one end and built-in benches around the walls. There was a reception desk behind a sliding-glass window, and we gave Tara's name to Sandy Brown, a young woman we were to come to know very well during the months ahead.

One by one the other families began to drift in until the room was crowded with parents and children. It was quite an assemblage. There were twenty-nine children being evaluated as new patients that week. They came from all over the United States and nine of them were from foreign countries.

The children came in all sizes and shapes and I'm sure that just about every bizarre behavior pattern on record was represented. There were some children who could talk, and some who couldn't; some who could walk, and others who couldn't. There were children who drooled and others whose mouths worked so poorly they could barely chew food. A few were screaming and yelling and running wildly through the room. Then there were others who lay quiet and immobile in their mothers' arms. One little girl spent the entire day tearing up paper into little pieces. Finally, there were several hyperactive little boys, whose behavior resembled Mark's.

Tara was the youngest one. A twenty-year-old veteran who had been shot in the brain during the Vietnam war was the oldest. The only thing these children had in common was that they were all brain-damaged. And probably the main thing the parents had in common was their determination to help their youngsters get well.

We had been there about thirty minutes when Tara's name was called and we were led down a narrow hall into a small room. There we were warmly greeted by a slight, elderly woman with a thick British accent, who was seated at a desk. We discovered that she was the wife of Professor Raymond Dart, the famous South African anthropologist.

"I'm to take Tara's history," she explained. "This will take quite a while, so make yourselves comfortable."

She then launched into a thorough questioning about all the events surrounding Donna's pregnancy and Tara's birth. Since they had been completely normal in every respect, we answered most of the questions with either yes or no and got through that section in no time.

Mrs. Dart was amazed. "It usually takes two or three hours to go through that portion," she marveled.

"That's okay," Donna replied. "But just wait until you get to the part that says 'Have there been any accidents?'—then we'll keep you busy!"

And we did spend several hours with Mrs. Dart before we had completed the history forms. By that time, lunch was being served. They had brought in big pots of homemade soup and stone-ground bread, butter, assorted cheese, and fruit. We all prepared TV trays and sat on the benches to eat. Some of the children could feed themselves and others, like Tara, had to be fed. Still others couldn't eat regular food at all and were given baby food.

We spent the rest of the day in the crowded reception area, waiting to be called into various evaluation rooms. Tara was tested in six areas of brain function in order to determine her condition, diagnosis, and neurological age. They checked her level of visual competence and they tested her auditory comprehension. They also checked her tactile competence, which falls into the area of touch. They then evaluated her mobility, her speech, and the degree to which she was able to use her hands.

The hours dragged by slowly. We were fed an excellent dinner around seven and still we were not finished. We found ourselves waiting some more. All the children were getting tired and cross. Tara fell asleep in my arms in between appointments.

Finally, at midnight, just when we were beginning to feel that the end would never come, we were called into the office of Mr. Glenn Doman, the director of the Institutes, and we knew this was to be our last appointment of the day. He was a stout man in his early fifties, with gray hair, twinkling blue eyes, and a jovial smile tucked in between his moustache and his beard. Donna whispered to me that she thought he looked like Santa Claus, and I had to agree.

He beamed at us and shook our hands. Then he said, "Congratulations! Your daughter is brain-injured! We're sorry she was hurt, but we feel we can help her." He spoke with us at great length about Tara. "She's our kind of kid," he said. "I've seen little tomatoes like her all over the world."

He said that because Tara had been born normal and had enjoyed two years of normality before her injury, she had an advantage over other children with similar injuries who had been affected from birth. Then he gave us his diagnosis.

"Tara has a profound bilateral diffuse midbrain injury. Profound refers to the degree of injury. Bilateral means that both sides of her brain are injured. Diffuse means that the injury is scattered rather than concentrated in one spot, and midbrain refers to the portion of the brain that is damaged. We don't know why, but all midbrain-injured kids are charming little con artists, just like your Tara. Right now, we are enjoying considerable success with midbrain injuries."

Then he went on to tell us of the long hours and hardships we would face if we decided to put Tara on their program. He concluded by outlining for us our schedule for the remaining four days. It was nearly two in the morning, and Donna and Tara and I were exhausted. Wearily, I drove us back to our hotel for some sleep before our nine o'clock appointment just a few hours away.

The next day included more of the same. Most of the parents were considerably more relaxed now. The Institutes accepts only brain-injured children, and on the first day many of the families were worried as to whether or not their children actually were brain-injured and whether or not the Institutes would accept them as patients. Of course, we had known Tara was brain-injured from the start, so we had been spared that worry.

This was a get-acquainted day. We parents felt free to talk with one another about ourselves and our children. Nearly a third of those present didn't speak English, which made conversation with them difficult, but we all did the best we could.

Tara went in to see the same people on Tuesday that she had seen on Monday, and they tested her still more thoroughly. We enjoyed another kettle of hot homemade soup for lunch but, fortunately, we were finished with our appointments before dinnertime. Donna, Tara, and I were all asleep early that night, trying to catch up on our rest.

The next two days, Wednesday and Thursday, were to be devoted to lectures to parents. The same staff that had evaluated the children on Monday and Tuesday would care for them on Wednesday and Thursday. This worked out nicely because they could observe them under more normal conditions rather than strictly in a test atmosphere. Donna and I left Tara in the reception area, confident that she would be well cared for.

Then we headed across the grounds to the Valentine Auditorium, where we were to spend the next ten hours listening to key staff members lecture. Everyone had brought jackets and blankets because the temperature in the auditorium is maintained at about 65° to keep the people awake. Donna, who is always warm, was delighted at the prospect of spending the day in a cold room.

The lectures proved to be fascinating. After all, they were talking about everyone's favorite subject—brain-injured children and how to make them well. We were all so spellbound I don't think anyone would have fallen asleep even if the room had been warmer.

Glenn Doman addressed us for about half the day and he proved to be an excellent speaker. He began talking about neurological organization. We found it extremely interesting because Tara had been through some of the stages he mentioned. He began with death, which has no neurological organization. Tara had been dead six different times so we certainly identified with that. After that he went through the dead person being revived and then being in a coma, which is really more like being dead than alive. We were quite familiar with this condition also. Then he discussed the various stages of consciousness through which we had seen Tara progress.

He spoke of being able to move and make sounds, and we remembered when Tara had been like that. He then went through the person being able to walk and talk, but poorly, and the next step upward, which he called Strauss's Syndrome—hyperactive and incoordinate. This described Mark perfectly.

The next stage was termed Delacato's Syndrome, signifying the individual who is unable to read due to poor neurological organization. Average came next, and then above average but with reading problems. Even these people they considered to have poor neurological organization due to a poor neurological environment.

Mr. Doman explained that on more than one occasion, they had taken a child through all of these steps of neurological organization. He said that the program our children would be embarking upon was a program of neurological organization, aimed at organizing their brains.

Brain injury is centered in the brain, he explained. It may affect the muscles, the child's legs may scissor, and he may be unable to function properly. But all the braces and surgery in the world cannot cure the problem because only the symptom is being treated, not the cause. The problem originates in the brain—to cure the problem, we must treat the brain.

"There will be failures," Mr. Doman explained. "There always are. And we have never been able to foretell who would fail and who wouldn't. We can have two profoundly injured children who seem to be identical in every way. And yet one will get well and one won't. We're just not smart enough to know why."

The entire two days were fascinating. Nobody had ever taken the time to explain things to us in such detail. By the time the lectures were over, Donna and I felt much more sure of ourselves and of what we wanted to do for Tara. We even had some new ideas for Mark. Tara had enjoyed her activities, too. In her usual delightful way, she had talked the staff members into spending the days talking to her and taking her for walks in her stroller.

I suppose big and little boys alike are smitten by a pretty face and a pair of flashing blue eyes. Add to that the sweetest of smiles, a soft feminine voice, and a helplessness that begs to be attended, and you've got a winning combination. Oh, what a charming little con artist, indeed!

After having had their program explained to us so well, Donna and I were now enthusiastic supporters of the Institutes' far-reaching ideas. They no longer seemed unconventional to us but, quite the contrary, seemed extremely scientific and reasonable. We could hardly wait for Friday when they would give us Tara's full program.

We began our fifth day there by once more going through a series of appointments with the various staff members. But this time, each one gave us something to do. It was so thrilling to think that at last we had a real program of things we could do to help Tara. We were to give her eye exercises to help her gain convergence of vision. Also, we were instructed to blink a flashlight on and off in her eyes in order to perfect the dilation and constriction of her pupils.

The program included four five-minute crawling patterns a day, to teach her how it feels to crawl. We were supposed to put ice cubes in her hands to help her learn to let go and open her hands. Showing her flash cards with the words written in big red letters was designed to teach Tara reading, while help in mastering math was expected to result from showing her cards with red dots on them.

We were told to restrict Tara's fluids to twenty ounces a day because this would help her brain to function better. She was also put on a strict program of nutrition by their nutrition consultant, Adelle Davis. She even had a special position to get into in bed at night.

They then gave us a series of six exercises to be performed sixteen times a day each. This would take eight hours a day to perform, and included: (1) Holding Tara by her feet and swinging her upside down for a minute. (2) Standing Tara on an inclined ladder for a minute. (3) Putting a plastic bag similar to an oxygen mask over Tara's face for a minute. This would force her to take deeper breaths and increase her lung capacity in addition to propelling more oxygen to her brain. (4) Swinging Tara back and forth while holding her arms and legs for one minute. (5) Making Tara climb down a series of three rounded, graduated steps. This let gravity help her down and also set up a stress situation, which they hoped would trigger her midbrain into action. (6) Assisting Tara to crawl on the floor for one minute.

Our last appointment that day was with Sandy Brown. She told us exactly where Tara stood in their developmental profile of neurological organization. In visual competence, Tara was operating at a level comparable to that of a seven-month-old baby. That is, she could appreciate detail within a configuration, such as recognizing faces.

Tara was at a three-year-old level—right where she should be—in auditory competence because she could understand two thousand words and simple sentences. But Tara still had a startle reflex like that of newborn infants. Whenever she heard a loud noise or thought she was going to fall, Tara would jump and throw her arms and legs into the air. Sometimes she would cry hysterically over it. Even though she knew it was a silly thing to do, she was helpless to stop it.

In the area of tactile competence, Tara was at a twelve-month level, having a tactile understanding of the third dimension in objects that appear to be flat. But she was only functional, or imperfect, in the appreciation of gnostic sensation, which has to do with being ticklish. She was also only functional in her babinski reflex—another characteristic of newborn babies. When we ran a thumb up the bottom of her foot, her toes involuntarily spread apart.

Tara was a total flop at mobility, scoring at a level below that of a newborn infant. Newborns have free movement of their arms and legs without moving their bodies. Tara did not.

However, in the language area, Tara was once more just where she should be, with a speaking vocabulary of approximately two thousand words, which she used in short sentences. Manual competence or hand function found her way down the list, again at a newborn level. A tiny infant has what is called a grasp reflex. If you put something in its hand, the hand will automatically grasp it and is unable to let go. Even if a hot burning coal were put into a baby's hand, he would just hold it until his hand burned up. Tara's hands were also like this.

Therefore, in the six areas of brain function, Tara was at

a three-year level in only two. These were understanding and speech. Donna and I felt that surely these were the two areas most needed to live a normal life and were pleased that Tara fell into the normal range. However, that still left her behind in the other four areas, and we were anxious to get to work on these deficiencies in brain function.

Sandy also outlined the goals they hoped Tara would achieve during the next two months. She was careful to explain that they set their goals high and didn't necessarily expect Tara to have reached all of them by her next visit. Her goals were:

(1) Reading.
(2) Stereognosis, or the ability to tell by touch alone what is in your hand.
(3) The ability to stand on an inclined ladder at an increased angle, hopefully 75°.
(4) The ability to move down descending rounded steps.

"You don't think Tara might be crawling in two months?" Donna asked, disappointedly.

"No, I think it will be some time before Tara can crawl," was Sandy's frank reply.

It was late afternoon when Donna, Tara, and I piled into the car and headed back to Summit, New Jersey. We were in high spirits, and I think the greatest thing the Institutes had done for us that week was to give us hope. At long last, we had found someone who cared, someone who saw Tara not as a lifelong helpless cripple but as a beautiful little girl with a God-given potential to achieve.

8

Patterns for Progress

The car was full of happy chatter as we made the two-hour drive back to Tucker's house. Mark ran out to meet us and we gathered him up in our arms, savoring this brief moment of affection. We had missed him and it was a time of joyful reunion for all of us.

The following day we loaded up suitcases, souvenirs, and children and boarded the large jet that would take us back home. Donna and I used our time on the plane to think realistically about the Institutes and their program. They had promised us nothing but years of hard work, and yet we felt that in this work lay the key that could some day unlock the chains that kept Tara's body in prison. It was a tough game we were playing, but we were playing to win. What better way could we spend our lives than to use the time that was available to us to make our daughter well? And if we didn't succeed, at least we would know in our hearts that we had tried our best.

The next few days were hectic. School was starting for Mark and we were so thankful that our district had initiated a class for him locally so that Donna didn't have to drive him into Orange each day. We now had to arrange to have Tara's equipment built, and somewhere find the hundred helpers who would be required to put Tara through her daily routine.

We praised God for the wonderful friends He had given us to help us in our task. The day after our return, Margo had a lovely luncheon at her home for Donna and Tara. All of the women who had been helping before were invited and many brought friends.

Donna explained to them the nature of the work carried out by the Institutes, and revealed exactly what we were hoping to accomplish for Tara. Then she told them about the tremendous need for volunteers. It was a program that required more than one person to execute. Donna, of course, would work eight hours a day, seven days a week. But that was not enough. For two hours each day, she would need two other women to help her put Tara through her crawling patterns. For the other six hours each day, she would need one other woman to help her with Tara's frequency program. The response was overwhelming. Every woman there signed up for at least an hour a week to help. But even this did not satisfy the need, so we turned to the churches and newspapers for additional aid.

One newspaper article asking for help appeared in the *Saddleback Valley News,* and was written by their editor, Annette McCluskey. It began by saying in part:

Tara Nason is an alert, blue-eyed three-year-old, whose ever-ready smile would captivate the hardest of hearts and whose courage would defy the imagination. She's a pretty, intelligent brunette, who looks like any other young, three-year-old lady should, but there the similarities end. Tara can't play, she can't hold her dolls, she can't jump rope or skip down the street, she can't walk or do any of the things little girls do. . . .

We were both thrilled and amazed at the overwhelming response to our need. In a matter of days we had all the helpers our busy schedule required—men and women, girls and boys ranging from ten to seventy-five years of age. Our lives have been continuously enriched by hundreds of compassionate people willing to help someone less fortunate. We have often said that some of the nicest people in Mission Viejo are the ones who come through our front door every day of the week.

The initiation of Tara's program made necessary still more adjustments in our family life. Donna and I were especially concerned with Mark. How could we give this little dynamo of ours the time, attention, and love that he so desperately needed? Donna tried to spend time with him while Tara was napping. They played ball or talked. Occasionally Donna would get a sitter for Tara and take Mark horseback riding or treat him to a trip for ice cream. We tried to save one evening a week for Mark and would take him out for hamburgers or to a movie.

His teachers just couldn't seem to find the correct place for Mark in school. They felt he really was too advanced for the special class he was in, but the regular first grade classes they tried didn't seem to work out either. They finally placed him in a regular kindergarten class during the morning and put him into the special education class in the afternoon. He appeared to do well in kindergarten, and Donna and I were thrilled. Maybe, we told ourselves, Mark was going to be able to handle school sooner than we thought.

For all his boisterousness, he was a sensitive child and felt deeply for others. One evening, his blue eyes looked grave and his face wrinkled in a frown.

"Daddy, there's a little girl in my class who can't talk. Isn't that sad? Why? Why can't she talk?"

I cleared my throat and took a deep breath. "Mark," I paused, "I don't know why she can't talk. But I do know that God loves her just the way she is and that He has a wonderful plan for her life. He doesn't want you to feel sorry for her. He wants you to love her just like He does. Can you do that?" Mark looked serious, "I guess so."

During our first two months on the Institutes' program, we found out just how hard we could work and just how many activities we could squeeze into the hours of a day. We would often stop to marvel, wondering what we had done previously with all our time.

We were up early each day, getting the children ready. To save Donna time, I began to cook breakfast for the family. Together we would make the beds, and while Donna was feeding Tara and supervising Mark, I started the laundry. Then I would go off to work and Mark would catch the bus and be off to school. Shortly afterward, Tara's first helper would arrive, and she and Donna then launched the day's busy round of activities.

Tara normally began at eight-thirty with a half hour of her frequency program, which at that time included swinging upside down, standing on the inclined ladder, masking, and swinging by her arms and legs, eye exercises, crawling down the graduated steps called boulders, and assisted crawling.

At nine more volunteers would arrive, and Tara would add a five-minute crawling pattern to the frequency program each half hour, doing four patterns by eleven, in addition to her other exercises. The crawling pattern took three people to perform. Tara would lie prone on her padded table, while the three women assembled around it. One person would stand at Tara's head in order to turn it back and forth. Another one would move one arm and leg, and Donna would move the other arm and leg. They would move Tara in an exaggerated crawling motion in an attempt to teach her brain how it feels to crawl.

Tara was not particularly fond of patterning, but she tolerated it. Her little arms and legs were so stiff that moving them in the synchronized pattern was no easy task.

Singing and reciting nursery rhymes seemed to make things go better for everyone. Tara, who loves to sing, but can't carry a tune, always knows all the words. Whenever anyone would say the words incorrectly, Tara would be sure to set them straight.

By eleven, the day's patterns completed, Tara would continue with her frequency sequences. Donna also worked her math and reading programs into the day, popping up with a word or a page of dots in between exercises. They ate a hasty lunch from twelve to twelve-thirty, and then started back to work. Tara normally took from two to four off for an afternoon nap, which made a nice break for both her and Donna. However, those last three hours from four to seven really left Donna exhausted. Not Tara, though. She was as bright at seven in the evening as she was the first thing in the morning.

We had wondered how she would take to the vigorous exercise program, but we needn't have worried. Tara took it in stride, as she had all the other events in her short life. She enjoyed most of her exercises so much that she would cry "Don't stop" when they were over.

In the evening, after dinner, Donna brought in a little sack filled with various items for Tara to feel. Maybe there would be a marble, or a doll shoe, or a penny. She would put each one into Tara's hand and let her feel every part of it. Then she would see if Tara could identify the object by touch alone. Tara called it her sack game and enjoyed it immensely.

There was usually a story for the two children before bed. Tara was tucked in first and had to be positioned. One night she had her right leg bent at a right angle, her right arm up, and her head turned toward the right. The next night she would have her left leg bent, her left arm up, and her head turned toward the left. The Institutes called this the homolateral sleep position. I don't think Tara stayed in this position more than five minutes, but at least she started out that way.

One night in October, Donna had exciting news for me when I got home. "Tara crawled today! She really did!"

"All by herself?" I asked incredulously.

"Yes," came Tara's clear treble. "Wanna see?"

"I sure do," I said with real enthusiasm.

"Okay," Tara said, flashing me a proud smile.

One at a time, she painstakingly brought both hands up just above her head on the floor, a procedure which took about ten minutes. Then, with incredible concentration, she slowly pulled them down and her body slid over them. The entire production for one crawl forward took about fifteen minutes and then she started over again. Two crawls were about all she could manage before she crumpled into an exhausted heap on the floor, every muscle shaking from over-exertion. I realized that I was shaking, too—that my body had fought along with hers every inch of the way.

"Oh, Tara," I cried, gathering her up in my arms and smothering her with well-deserved kisses. "You crawl so well, it's a shame you're so ugly."

"I'm not ugly!" she shrieked in delight.

Another major step Tara made that fall was in the area of toilet training. She had originally been trained early and easily at the age of twenty months, but the accident had erased all traces of this ability, thrusting her back to pre-infancy habits in one fell swoop. Now, however, Donna was making excellent progress in her attempt to train Tara again and it looked as though she was finally out of daytime diapers for good.

Tara was progressing well on the inclined ladder, too. We had started her out with the ladder nearly horizontal. We would slip her feet into a lower rung and stretch her arms up over her head and help her to grasp a rung there. Originally, she was practically lying on the ladder, but as it became easier for her, we began raising the ladder to a steeper incline. It was hard work for her, and being the clever little con artist that she is, she used every trick in the book to get out of it.

One favorite diversion for Donna and Tara has been the Thursday lunches with Bobbie and Christie Merritt. Each Thursday they meet in a nearby restaurant for some relaxation and companionship. The two little girls chat while their mothers share the trials and tribulations known only to parents of brain-damaged children. Tara and Christie have formed what we hope will be a lasting friendship, built on mutual interest and concern.

One of the promises put forth in the Bible is that God will provide us with our needs even before we ask Him to. This has been our experience many times. As part of the Institutes program, we were supposed to return to Philadelphia for a one-day appointment once every two months, and our November visit was fast approaching. One of our wonderful volunteers was Wilma Chain, the wife of a lieutenant colonel in the Marines. One day she told Donna that her husband Bill's parents lived in Ardmore, a suburb of Philadelphia, and at her request they had agreed to take us in as house guests during Tara's revisits.

And so it was that Charles Chain met Tara and me as we alighted from our plane in Philadelphia. A tall, thin man, with white hair worn in a crewcut, his friendly smile soon put us at ease. He and his charming wife Libby were retired and lived in a lovely old home with their widowed daughter Sue and her two youngsters, Wendy and Craig. Tara immediately fell in love with the entire family and was calling them Grandma and Grandpa Chain before the night was out.

Charles drove us to the Institutes early the next morning. It was like returning to the home of an old and dear friend as I carried Tara into the reception area.

"Oh no, it can't be! It is! It's that ugly Tara Nason again!" Art Sandler bent down to give her a kiss and a pat as he passed busily through the room.

Tara was delighted and snuggled into my arms. As for me, I was excited and nervous. We had worked so hard these past two months. Would they be pleased with Tara's progress?

The room was soon filled with its customary assortment of brain-injured children. Many of them I remembered from the previous visit. Everyone was curious, anxious to see how the other families were doing. Did they have enough help? How many hours a day did they work? Had they noticed any progress? It took me some time to realize that the little girl playing quietly on the floor was the one who had liked to shred paper. I could imagine the joy of her parents at this change in behavior.

One by one, we were called into the different offices for Tara to be evaluated by the staff. I tape-recorded everything for Donna, who had stayed at home with Mark. They first took a complete history of everything that had happened to Tara during the two months since her last visit. Then they checked her in the six areas of brain function. She was also weighed and had every conceivable part of her body measured. Most brain-injured children do not grow as well as they should, so the Institutes was interested in this area of development.

Every time we went into someone's office for an appointment, I knew what to expect from Tara. First she wanted a pencil and paper so she could "write." When she had grown tired of that, she would suddenly have a desperate urge to go potty. The irritating thing about taking Tara to the bathroom is that sometimes she will perform and sometimes she won't. And there is no way of discerning her sincerity in advance. Needless to say, we became well acquainted with the Institutes' facilities that day.

After we had made the rounds and eaten lunch, we started over again. This time, each staff member made adjustments in Tara's program. Finally, at the end of a long day, we were called into Sandy Brown's office. Sandy would go over Tara's progress report with us and outline her new program.

This was the moment I had been waiting for. My throat was dry. I moistened my lips and swallowed hard.

"Tara has done remarkably well over the past two months," she began. "Whereas in September, Tara visually was operating at a seven-month level, she can now read and has risen to a six-year-old level. Although she still doesn't have the freedom of movement present in a newborn baby, she has begun to crawl and has moved up to a 2.5-month level in mobility."

By now, I was so thrilled I could barely sit still. My smile broadened as I thought of how happy Donna would be when I told her.

"By the way," Sandy continued. "For all practical purposes, Tara shouldn't be able to crawl. She's much too stiff. She is moving by sheer willpower, forcing her cortex to assume a function that rightfully belongs to the pons.

"Her hand function is much better, also. She has lost her grasp reflex and now has vital release which is recorded at 2.5 months on the profile. In all, she has gained 4.1 months in neurological age over the past two months, a rate that is 205 percent of average.

"Tara has also done well developmentally," Sandy said. "She has gained weight, and her chest and head have grown much faster than average."

Then she turned to Tara. "Tara, you're excellent. You tell your mommy she's doing a good job, okay?"

"Okay," Tara responded, obviously pleased with herself. I was virtually tingling with excitement. Tara really was improving. We had felt it, but to have the Institutes agree with us had been almost too much to hope for. I could just picture Donna's delight when I told her.

Tara and I made a happy pair the next day as we once more boarded the plane that would take us back to California. We were really becoming members of the jet set.

Tara was dressed in a red knit dress with white tights and had a red ribbon in her almost-shoulder-length brown hair. Her beauty, combined with her helplessness, always attracted a great deal of attention and this was no exception. As the stewardesses gathered around to admire her, I made a mental note to explore with Donna any way that we might be able to devise to counteract all the attention she received.

One Sunday in December, Margo and Gary Clarke came over and spent the whole day doing Tara's program. Donna, Mark, and I went to Disneyland. What a great day, and how nice it was to be free of responsibility for eight whole hours. Mark loved it, and it was so good for him to be the center of attention for awhile. The park was remarkably uncrowded, so we really got to do a lot of things. We even managed several rides on the Matterhorn bobsleds, which are Mark's favorites.

When we arrived home, we were relieved to find that Tara had done fine without us. "I'm fantastic!" she said, and then added, "Gary taught me that."

That evening we met another couple with a brain-injured child—a lovely twelve-month-old baby girl who had suffered an attack of spinal meningitis in May. We tried to give them some hope and offered some suggestions for therapy. They were the first in a long line of parents who have come to us for help through the years. We families with brain-injured children have a virtual underground subculture. Sooner or later we meet each other to compare notes and exchange ideas.

Some of the parents we have come to know have been pleased with their child's progress and with the therapy he receives at the local rehabilitation clinics. Others have been dissatisfied with their child's progress and are eagerly looking for more help, determined couples with a real drive for success.

That Monday, Tara's new equipment was installed and she started her new program. It was more extensive than the first, but she and Donna really enjoyed the change. Her swings had been replaced by an upside-down hanging program. We had had straps made to loop over Tara's shoes, and then we slipped the straps over hooks that were suspended from a beam in the hallway ceiling. We were to work her up to hanging upside down for four minutes at a time. She wasn't terribly crazy about the idea but tolerated it fairly well and did her best to twist from side to side and to lift her legs up and down at Donna's request.

Tara's inclined ladder was gradually being adjusted to being more and more vertical, and she could sometimes stand and hold on for fifteen seconds at a time, which was very encouraging. Her crawling was also improving. However, it was so difficult for her and required so much concentration that we tried everything we could think of to motivate her. Donna would get down on the floor and crawl with her or make her dolls crawl with her. There always had to be some objective for which she could aim—a toy or a glass of milk. Tara did very little spontaneous crawling—mainly, I think, because it was such a difficult chore. Also, because of her poor hand coordination, she really couldn't do anything with a toy even if she crawled over to it.

Now that December was in full swing, we were busy preparing for Christmas. Mark and Tara were breathless with anticipation. Donna and I had finally come to grips with the fact that the old Tara of Christmas 1969 was gone forever, and this year we hardly thought of her at all. The new Tara

was a delight to us all, her deep-blue eyes bright with excitement.

We were especially thrilled because Donna's parents were
coming to spend a week with us. The four months since we
had seen them added up to the longest period of time that
Donna had ever been separated from them.

As the big day drew near, Tara began receiving gifts from
her wonderful helpers. Most were even thoughtful enough
to bring something for Mark, too. And this generous out-
pouring of love has been present every Christmas since then.

Christmas Eve was wet. In fact, it had rained for three
days, which is very unusual in our part of the country. We
were surprised to see a car pull up in front. In California,
people don't get out much in the rain. It turned out to be
the president of the local YMCA Men's Club, his wife, and
his granddaughter. They had brought Tara a gift from their
organization, a most beautiful doll. The kindness they
showed to one less fortunate filled our whole day with sunshine.

One day, shortly before Christmas, the largest of our local
newspapers had called to ask if they could do a feature story
about Tara. In contrast to previous articles in other papers,
which dealt mainly with our plight and the need for help,
this one would be strictly human interest. The result was a
large story and picture on the front page of the Christmas
Eve edition.

The tale of our little miracle girl and all the volunteers
who came regularly to help her get well would have touched
the heart of Scrooge himself. Donna even received a phone
call from a woman whose son had been brain-injured. She
had been praying for knowledge of a place to take him for
treatment. We quickly informed her about our very encouraging experiences at the Institutes in Philadelphia and

recommended that they write for an appointment for the boy.

With so many people coming daily to our home, Donna and I decided that here was a perfect opportunity to let others know what God was doing in our lives. So we got an ichthus sign to put on our front door. It is in the shape of a fish with the Greek letters I-X-O-Y-E, which mean Jesus Christ, Son of God, Savior. Since the first century, Christians have used it to identify themselves. Donna was always being asked how she managed to do all the things she did, and she wanted to advertise the source of her power. Today we have a large poster on the door to Tara's workroom that reads "Jesus Power."

The week after Christmas, Tara's left leg began to act up. Suddenly she could no longer kick it up and down while hanging. In addition, it was not bearing weight properly when she stood on her ladders. It bent out in front at the knee, thus forcing her right knee out in back. Donna was afraid her hip was becoming dislocated, and she was proved to be right. X rays showed a partial dislocation of the left hip.

This had been an ever-present possibility for a long time, but the reality of it left us stunned and unprepared. Now what were we going to do? Tara's adductor muscles, which are the ones on the inside of her legs, are too strong. They are what make her legs scissor, and the constant pulling of these muscles and the shallowness of her hip socket enabled the head of the femur to slide partially out of place.

The orthopedic surgeon wanted to put casts on her legs, which would hold them apart in a frog position. After two or three years of this, he felt the hip socket would be properly formed again and the femur would be in place. The end result of such a procedure was only too obvious to Donna and me.

If Tara's legs were held motionless for two or three years, there would be nothing left of them with which to work. There would be no hope of her ever walking again. We had seen the wasted, bony legs of those who were unable to use them. This was definitely not what we wanted for Tara. Her legs were shapely and well-formed, as was the rest of her body, and we intended to keep them that way.

Dr. Coster, her neurosurgeon, had told us that if we were not on the extensive therapy program, Tara's healthy body would be withered and bent like a pretzel. We knew that casting was not the answer, but what was? We were soon to find out that nobody really has the answer.

There is a surgical procedure that can reshape the hip socket and put the femur in place, but that does nothing for the adductors, which caused the problem in the first place. They would only begin pulling away again and ruin the new hip socket. And it was Tara's brain that caused the adductors to be too strong, so we were right back where we started.

Talk about a vicious circle! We decided that the only thing to do was to keep working with the Institutes and hope that we could change Tara's brain.

Tara's next appointment was January 12, and we decided that Donna would take her and that I would stay home with Mark. She would make the trip with Melinda Stroschein and Curt. Two-and-a-half-year-old Curt is a profoundly injured athetoid, which means that instead of his body being rigid like Tara's, it is limp. At that time, he had very little speech and experienced great difficulty holding up his head. Taking care of him was quite a task for Melinda who, in addition, was two months pregnant and nauseated.

Neither Donna nor Melinda had ever really traveled without their husbands. I don't know about Melinda, but Donna was petrified. I'm afraid it was rather like the blind leading the blind. Donna related to me later that they made quite a spectacle upon disembarking in Philadelphia. Two relatively small women trying to carry two heavy nonsitting children, two small suitcases, two large purses, and four heavy coats has got to be quite a sight.

They were late arriving at the airport to catch their plane home, and ran all the way from the entrance to the airline gate. Poor Melinda, in her condition, dropped breathlessly to the floor in front of the desk. She was all right, just exhausted from running with her arms full, but Donna told me it nearly scared her to death.

Tara had another good report at the Institutes. She had moved up to her age level—three years—in the area of tactile competence, having attained the goal of stereognosis. She was now exactly where she should be in every phase of neurological development, with the exception of mobility and hand function. These would be her weak points.

Glenn Doman had carefully explained to Donna that progression on the profile would be painfully slow from now on. Tara would crawl, but only functionally, and it would be years before she could get up on her hands and knees to creep. Her hand function would be equally slow. We must now work on quality, being content with the necessary improvements that must come before Tara could move up on their charts.

They gave us another backbreaking program, and we set to work. There was no doubt about it, the dislocated hip had interfered with function and therefore with progress.

But Donna, Tara, and I trusted God and more and more came to trust in Him to work things out.

We often took the children out to dinner. Tara usually sat next to Donna in the booth, leaning against her so she wouldn't fall. For months, she had been asking for a spoon to hold when we were in a restaurant. We usually told her no, because holding the spoon made her lose her sitting balance. Instead of bringing the spoon to her mouth, she would lean over and take her mouth to the spoon. We felt this would contribute to poor posture. Periodically we let her have one, but the results were always the same.

One night in February, we were seated in a booth at our favorite coffee shop when Tara began insisting that we give her a spoon. To everyone's delight, she began carefully and thoughtfully to bring the spoon up to her mouth, lick it, and put it back in her lap. When her dinner came, she insisted upon putting a french fry on the spoon. Naturally it fell right off because she wasn't able to balance it correctly.

We were about to give up when Mark said, "Why don't you try a fork?"

We did—and it worked. Tara fed herself her whole dinner —half a hamburger and some french fries—with that fork, never once lowering her head. Of course, Donna had to put the food on the fork, but we were so thrilled. At last, the thought of self-feeding didn't seem quite so remote. It would take years of practice, we knew, but the first step had been taken.

By May, Tara had reached another milestone in her young life: she had learned to roll over both from front to back and from back to front. But, probably, the most important thing that happened that month was that both Mark and Tara committed their young lives to Jesus.

Mark had been questioning us for some time. "What makes you a Christian? Can I be one too? I love Jesus, you know."

Donna and I had considered him too young to make such a serious decision and had mistakenly put him off on the matter. Then Donna read a book that set us straight. The next time Mark brought up the subject, Donna was ready for him. We both felt that he fully understood what he was doing and we have both witnessed the change in him since his new birth.

We call him the neighborhood evangelist because he is so interested in winning new souls for Jesus. It was six-and-one-half-year-old Mark who led three-and-one-half-year-old Tara to the saving cross of Christ.

"Do you want Jesus to live in your heart?" he asked her one evening.

"Yes," she replied, and the two of them called Donna in to explain it to Tara and to help them with their prayer. It was with much joy that I received the day's news that night.

That spring brought yet another loss to our family. My father was transferred, and he and my mother moved to Saratoga, a picturesque suburb of San Francisco. In less than a year, both sets of our parents had left the area. Never again would our children know the closeness of grand-parents.

For months Donna had been looking forward to a long visit with her parents. Since July was my busy time, she and the children left for Texas right after school was out for Mark. In the twelve years we had known each other, Donna and I had never been separated for as long as a month and that part of it we approached with some trepidation. Little did we realize that before the month was out I would be joining Donna at Tara's bedside in a Houston hospital.

9

Tara for Others

I really missed Donna and the children even though I was working fairly long hours and wasn't home much. It is so lonely to come home every night to an empty house. We talked often by phone, and this was usually the high spot of my day.

For Donna, it was wonderful just to be with her family. Nassau Bay, Texas, is the home of many of our nation's astronauts. It is a lovely community perched on the flat coastal plain and bordered by the Gulf of Mexico. That summer it proved to be a town with a heart as more than seventy-five of its citizens volunteered to help put Tara through her exercise program. Even the wife of one of the lunar astronauts turned out to help us.

Unfortunately, the trip was marred by illness. First Mark had tonsillitis and an ear infection, then Tara wound up with tonsillitis and an ear infection. Next Tara, Donna, and her mother and father had the flu. For several months, Tara had been suffering from bladder infections. She had developed one right after another. So it wasn't surprising that she came down with one again. When Donna went over Tara's history with the urologist, he suggested that Tara be put in the hospital for complete testing to see what was causing all the infections.

Donna and I were skeptical. We wanted very much to know the cause of Tara's chronic problem, but were afraid that the experience in the hospital might be too traumatic for her. After all, she was only four years old and had already suffered more than many people do in a lifetime. We weighed the alternatives in prayer and decided to go ahead. The tests were scheduled for July 6, and I decided to fly down to assist Donna.

Herman Hospital in Houston has a wonderful pediatrics program. It requires that the mother room in with the child. The children feel more secure, and the nurses are freed from baby-sitting to do more important chores. It was an ideal situation for Tara and worked very well.

She hated the X rays as we knew she would. There was something about lying flat on her back on that hard table with the big X-ray machine directly overhead that terrified Tara. She began to scream hysterically as soon as we placed her on the table and didn't stop until the ordeal was over.

At this time, she always had what appeared to be one continuous startle reflex—her arms and legs rigid and thrown up into the air. Donna and I pleaded and begged and used force in an effort to keep Tara still and in a proper position for X rays. The close of the session found all three of us dripping with perspiration and completely exhausted.

Later on, as they prepared Tara for exploratory surgery,

Donna and I tried our best to remain calm and unworried. For two people who were deeply concerned, I guess we put up a pretty good front. Tara wasn't at all worried as she lay on the table waiting to go into the operating room. They had given her medication to make her drowsy, and we hoped that it would put her to sleep before they wheeled her away from us. But Tara wasn't about to be put out that easily. She talked a blue streak, even though the drug had made her tongue thick and practically useless, and her eyes fluttered as she struggled to keep them open.

As they took her into surgery, Donna and I were left to wait and wonder. The anesthetic made Tara dreadfully ill. She was nauseated for nearly twenty-four hours, retching violently. We didn't dare leave her for a moment for fear she would choke to death. But with the amazing resiliency of children, she was bright and talkative the next morning. As we prepared to leave, Tara began to complain. "I don't want to go home yet. I want to ride on the table again. That was fun!"

Later on, the doctor explained to us what he had discovered. We had known all along that Tara's arms and legs were being held rigid by her brain. The doctor found that some of her internal equipment was also impaired due to the brain damage, as was the case with her urinary tract. He had dilated her while she was under anesthesia and this temporarily helped the problem, but it was by no means a cure. The cure to this, as well as to Tara's other problems, lay locked in her brain.

Tara's July report at the Institutes mirrored our own feelings. She had not achieved much progress since her May visit. The illnesses had taken their toll. I think even Tara was disgruntled.

"I go to the Institutes for startle reflex," she said disgustedly. "I startle when the door opens, and I startle when it closes. Good grief, Charlie Brown!"

We returned to California with renewed determination to get better results with her therapy patterns in the interval before our next trip to Philadelphia. However, working with Tara became increasingly difficult for Donna because she had become pregnant. We were both stunned and delighted at the prospect of another baby. Donna had been wanting one since before Tara's accident, but the intensity of her program had made the thought of another child out of the question.

In the first place, we knew we couldn't afford one. The trips to Philadelphia kept the family coffers empty. Our home was too small; the tiny bedrooms were full. Even the ten-by-ten fourth bedroom was crowded with the ladders and various other pieces of equipment that were required for Tara's therapy. The eight hours a day, seven days a week that Donna spent with Tara just didn't leave her any time to care for a baby. Not to mention the fact that Tara was heavy, and the patterning program itself was very physical and required a great deal of strength to perform. No, we had long ago decided, we couldn't possibly have a baby. Maybe some day later, when Tara was well.

I suppose we would have gone on like that forever, had God not stepped in and decided to bless us in this very special way.

Because we had seen so many damaged children in our wanderings with Tara, Donna and I were especially concerned that our baby be healthy and well. In addition, we were hoping that the baby would be a girl. While we enjoyed a special relationship with Tara, we had missed so many of the little-girl things we had always anticipated.

For Tara, there would be no ballet recitals. Because of

her therapy, even her clothing was limited. Perhaps we could all share in these things through another daughter. Donna added a new prayer to her list each day, asking God that if it be His will He might give us a healthy baby girl. And almost to herself, she would add, "and please let her be blond like me."

Our niece Marjorie was to be confirmed in the Episcopal Church one Sunday, so we all drove to my sister Gale's house in Palos Verdes for the occasion. The lovely sanctuary that had been our church home for so many years was filled to capacity with confirmees and their families. The lights were dimmed and all was quiet when Donna noticed that Tara was all bent over, her head practically hanging in her lap.

"Tara!" she whispered, "sit up!"

Tara looked up, gave Donna a look of total disgust, and in a voice to match said, "But, Mommy, can't you see I'm praying?"

It had been nearly two years since Donna and I had received Christ into our lives and yet we had not found a permanent church home. We felt God was calling us to do so now and enrolled in Pastor's Classes at the Presbyterian Church of the Master in Mission Viejo. Soon we were warmly received into that friendly group of believers.

When their youth department said it would be pleased to accept Tara in its Sunday school program, it was almost too good to be true. We shuffled her schedule around and arranged to attend church as a family every other Sunday. These hours spent in the worship of our Lord have been a wonderful blessing for all of us.

That fall I was involved in staging a dinner for a community fund-raising project.

"You'll need someone to give the invocation," Donna reminded me. "Why don't you ask Dr. Schuller?"

We often watched Dr. Robert H. Schuller's church services, which were telecast each Sunday on a program called "Hour of Power." The Garden Grove Community Church was located only thirty miles away.

To our surprise and pleasure, Dr. Schuller accepted the invitation, and he and his charming wife were among the first guests to arrive. He is a tall, distinguished-looking man, with steel-gray hair and eyes that twinkle from behind his glasses. His wife Arvella, a petite and gracious woman, stood quietly by his side.

Donna and I hastened over to introduce ourselves and to help them feel at home. There was the usual small talk, and then Dr. Schuller stunned us by asking me if I would like to assist him on a project in which he was intimately involved. As he told me later, he had acted on an impulse that he believed had come from the Holy Spirit, God's helping Spirit here on earth.

A few days later, in a meeting with Dr. Schuller in the Tower of Hope, located on the grounds of the Christian church he pastors, he told me he would like me to become associated with him in some way. Would I help him with some special projects as a volunteer? I had always wanted to serve God in a more concrete way, and agreed to assist Dr. Schuller in his campaign to help free the many pastors who are tortured and imprisoned behind the Iron Curtain.

Meanwhile, Donna and I were more and more concerned about our small home and the impending blessed event in our family. How ever would we find room? We investigated the costs of adding on an extra room, but they were phenomenal. It seemed that buying a new home was the only answer. After much prayer and soul-searching we decided to step out in faith and purchase one of the new homes being built in our area.

In Mission Viejo, buying a new home isn't always easy. They put houses on sale in units of forty-five about once a month. There are usually 100 to 150 families who want to buy the forty-five houses, so the Mission Viejo Company operates on what they call a lottery system. They assign each family a number, then place all the numbers in a bowl, and draw them out one by one. If someone else's number is called first and they want to buy the same lot and house you do, then of course they buy it and you are out of luck. We knew of several couples who had been to as many as three or four drawings and still hadn't been able to purchase a house.

With a new baby due in April, we didn't have time to try several lotteries. The next one was scheduled in two weeks, with houses due for completion in May. By then, the baby would be born. The thought of moving and maintaining Tara's program and caring for a new infant all at the same time was horrifying. Yet, it seemed to be the only choice available to us. We examined the lot sites available and didn't like any of them.

Then, one Sunday afternoon, Donna suggested that we see if there were any lots left from the unit that had been offered for sale a month earlier.

"Are you kidding?" I chided her. "You know there are never any left over."

But she was insistent, so I made a telephone check. I could hardly believe it when the salesman told me there were two lots left.

We raced over right away. One of the lots was perfect for us. It had a small front yard, a relatively large backyard, and no steep banks. As we reserved our lot at the sales office,

Donna and I could only praise God for this unlikely turn of events. Who would have thought we would be able to buy the lot we wanted without going through a lottery? And, as an extra bonus, this house would be completed in February! There would be time to get settled before the arrival of our new baby.

We had a very pregnant household that fall. Both Donna and our Himalayan cat, Snowball, were expecting. The kittens were due around the first of December, and Mark and Tara were spellbound. The big event found all four of us crammed into our tiny laundry room.

While Snowball labored and delivered four beautiful long-haired kittens, we watched in total fascination. We all felt very close to God as we marveled at His infinite care, which is so clearly manifested in birth.

Tara felt herself quite the maternity expert by this time, and was conducting guided tours of the feline nursery every hour on the hour. With the arrival of each helper, she would launch into her spiel.

"Snowball had her kittens, and I watched. They came right out of her tummy. My mommy has a baby in her tummy, too. And someday when I'm big I'm going to have one, too."

Donna and I would exchange glances about this time. Would Tara ever be well enough to have children?

That Christmas brought a special friend for a return visit —Santa Claus! Jim Cooper, a Los Angeles TV reporter, donates a lot of time each year to visiting shut-in children in our area. Mark had just learned the sad truth about Santa, and it was quite a traumatic experience for him. Tara was still a believer, though, and greeted his jingling bells with wide-eyed wonder.

Santa was pleased to note how much better Tara's balance was and how nicely she was holding herself. She was wearing her burgundy velvet Christmas dress and in the interests of cleanliness didn't get down on the floor to demonstrate her improved crawling.

Donna had just gone nonstop from morning sickness (which she had all day) to indigestion (which she also had all day). She was also experiencing the customary backaches that go along with pregnancy. It hurt me to think of her constant task of programming Tara eight hours a day, but she rarely complained and seemed to take it all in stride.

"Just wait until I get too fat to reach the patterning table," she joked.

Fortunately, that day never came.

I also have trouble with my back. Poor Tara knew that it hurt both Donna and me to carry her, and every time we picked her up she would ask guiltily, "Does your back hurt today?"

One day during Christmas vacation, Mark brought a neighbor boy in the house to play. I had seen him around before, but he was not a regular visitor. They had only been playing for fifteen minutes, when the child went home. Mark came storming into the room, his fists clenched and his face flushed.

"I told him to go home and never come back to my house again!" he said angrily. "He was making fun of Tara."

Well, I thought to myself. There has to be a first time for everything. But I was pleased with the way Mark had handled the situation and told him so. To my knowledge, that is the only time anyone has said anything cruel about Tara. I hope and pray that if and when the time comes, she will possess enough personal strength to defend herself against any onslaughts. She's a tough little girl and I think, with God's help, she'll be able to handle almost any situation that arises.

The most exciting thing to happen to Tara in the new year was that she started preschool at our church. Her whole face would light up, her blue eyes sparkling from behind their fringe of dark lashes, at the very mention of school. She attended for one hour each on Tuesday and Thursday mornings. Donna was willing to go with her at these times to help, but the staff wouldn't hear of it. Tina McKinley, the director, said Tara should come alone just like the other children.

"And send her in old clothes," she added. "She'll be painting, you know."

Tara was so proud and excited that first day I thought she would pop. Donna had washed her nearly waist-length hair and brushed it until it glistened. She wore it in twin pony-tails, tied with red grosgrain ribbons. Tara's face was flushed, her eyes shining, as Donna wheeled here in to class in her stroller. Every eye was fixed on Tara's laughing face, and before a word could be said she was surrounded by exuberant four-year-olds. As the "nap time" towel Margo had brought her so aptly expresses, "Happiness is being one of the gang."

As she related to me later, Donna gave Tara a quick kiss and told her she would pick her up at ten-thirty. With never a backward glance, Tara was already at a table, paint brush in hand.

That evening, Tina phoned to let us know how thrilled they were to have Tara in their class.

"First days are usually difficult for most children," she said enthusiastically, "but Tara joined right in. We had planned to take it slowly with her, but she was one step ahead of us all the way, even encouraging the other children to join in the activities."

Tara made some wonderful little friends that year and enjoyed the little-girl fun of birthday parties and school field trips.

The largest newspaper in Orange County is the *Santa Ana Register*. They had published an extensive article about Tara and her volunteers in November, and had been following her progress closely for some time. The *Register* prints a wonderful public service column each day called "The Troubleshooter." Through the Troubleshooter's Angels, this fine organization aids various civic endeavors within the county.

We were fortunate to be the recipient of their helping hand when they paid for Tara's February revisit to the Institutes. For the first time since her original evaluation, we were scheduled to stay for five days. The Institutes, we had discovered, rarely maintained the status quo for long. They were always looking for ways and means to make their program more effective in its treatment of brain-injured children. They had found five days of intensive therapy to be of great value, and were beginning to schedule children for appointments of this nature.

Tucker and Nancy had, by this time, moved to Cincinnati, Ohio, and were courageous enough to watch Mark for us for the week. We dropped him off with Tucker at the airport and continued on to New York City. Donna and I were especially excited about this trip. Like other parents of children with problems, we overlooked no opportunity for possible improvements.

I had read an article in *Newsweek* about Dr. Irving Cooper, who practiced neurosurgery at St. Barnabas Hospital for Chronic Diseases in New York. He had recently discovered a type of brain surgery in which he went into the skull and froze certain brain cells. This caused an instantaneous and complete reduction of spasticity in the muscles. Here was new hope! Tara's only remaining problem was spasticity or stiffness of the muscles, which made it nearly impossible for her to move.

I had called Dr. Cooper's office back in December, the day after I read the magazine article, and we had been given a 10:30 appointment on the Thursday morning before Tara's visit to the Institutes.

Now the anticipation was finally over; the day of reckoning had arrived. It was clear and bitterly cold that day, with a raw wind whipping in between the tall buildings. After circling the narrow, dim streets, we finally located St. Barnabas Hospital. It was a huge place, and we thought we would surely freeze before we arrived at the proper building.

Donna, seven months pregnant, was drained from her long plane trip and extremely nauseated. She quickly sank down in a chair in the doctor's sparsely furnished reception area.

"I'm Mr. Nason," I dutifully reported to the crisp-looking red-haired nurse, who received that bit of information with a blank look.

"From California," I ventured, "with my daughter Tara. She has an appointment at ten-thirty with Dr. Cooper."

A look bordering on frenzy appeared in the woman's eyes. "Today? With Dr. Cooper? Well, I just don't understand. He's not in town today. From California, did you say?" Her voice rising. "Did you come to New York from California just for this appointment?"

"Yes. We did." I said, trying to hide my disappointment. I glanced over at Donna, whose face was ashen but expressionless.

The poor woman was frantic, which made us feel somewhat better since we were, too. She finally located Tara's medical records. They had NO HELP written on them in big red letters. Our hearts just sank.

"Why?" I asked. "He hasn't even seen Tara yet. How does he know he couldn't help her?"

The nurse was scanning the records for some clue. "Oh, of course," she said after a moment. "She's too young. Dr. Cooper isn't doing the cryopulvenectomy on anyone under twelve years of age."

Donna and I both heaved a joint sigh of relief. "Could we talk to somebody about it?" I asked.

As it finally worked out, after waiting until three-thirty, we were able to see Dr. Armen, a physician on Dr. Cooper's staff. He was a small man and spoke with an accent. He smiled at Tara, asked her a few questions, and gave her a quick neurological examination.

"You're a lucky little girl," he began. "According to what I just read on your medical records, you shouldn't even be alive."

He then went on to tell us what we had traveled three thousand miles to learn. Their surgery could help Tara. She was, in fact, an excellent candidate. Her age was the only reason it wouldn't be advisable. There was some risk connected with the surgery because it involved the destruction of certain brain cells. That, coupled with the natural improvement of children in Tara's condition, made early surgery inadvisable.

Since Tara had once been normal and at one time knew how to use her muscles properly, and since Dr. Armen felt that she still knew how to use them properly, he thought the surgery would bring about a miraculous change in her. He told us, as we had been told before, that Tara has an overlay; that is, a layer of spasticity covers her muscles and prevents her from using them. Dr. Cooper's new surgery removes the overlay.

"If all our patients were like Tara," he said, "they would be on the road to recovery the day after surgery." He also told us of new discoveries they had made recently. "Time is in Tara's favor. By the time she is twelve, our procedures will be perfected. I think she has a bright future. Keep working with her as you are, maintaining her good muscle tone, until the time comes when we can help her."

Donna and I left New York City feeling elated. Even the graffiti-covered buildings didn't look quite so dingy. If we failed on the Institutes' program, it wasn't the end. There was at least this one more avenue to be explored. One way or another, Tara was going to make it!

After spending the weekend with my aunt and uncle, Kay and Clint Mesker, in Maplewood, New Jersey, we had the pleasure of visiting a friend of ours from high school days. Lee and her husband, Dave Bulfin, whom we met for the first time, live in Fords, New Jersey. As we enjoyed renewing an old friendship and starting a new one, it made us think of all the wonderful friends we had made through Tara. We marveled at the places we had been and the things we had done that would never have occurred had Tara not suffered that tragic accident.

I think it is very true that when God calls on us to suffer, He always provides the inner strength and the outward circumstances that so aptly help us through the ordeal. As that old proverb expresses so well, "When God closes a door, somewhere He opens a window."

On Sunday we drove down to Philadelphia to the Institutes. It was cold and raining and nearly dark when we arrived at the door of the old mansion on the Institutes' grounds that was to be our home for the next week. We soon discovered that it had been converted into a dormitory for some of the students who were taking advanced training there.

This stately home had so many rooms and halls that Donna never did learn her way around and kept getting lost each time she ventured alone from our quarters. They had assigned us two small rooms on the second floor, and we would share a bath with the other family that was staying there for the week.

The next morning at breakfast in the old dining room, we met Mark Hall and his mother and older brother. Mark, a normal child until the age of seven, when he had been in an automobile accident, was now sixteen. He had received profound neurological injuries and had improved very little since that tragic time.

Like so many individuals with brain injuries, he was unable to move or to talk. And since function determines structure, his mouth and teeth and his body itself had become deformed over the years. His eyes seemed bright, though, and we were convinced that he understood what was said. Here was yet another child robbed of his birthright because of brain injury.

Tara liked Mark right away. She didn't seem to mind that he didn't return her conversation, but chattered away at him all day. They were working side by side, which delighted Tara, and she would call out words of encouragement to Mark as he went through his program.

Those first two days, we didn't pattern Tara at all, just hung her upside down and masked her. Tara's old friend Art Sandler was in charge of the therapy, and he worked the two children very hard.

Art's boundless energy and enthusiasm never ceased to amaze me. It is obvious how very much he loves hurt children, and his dedication is a wonderful thing to see. I feel certain that if Art lived at our house and supervised Tara's therapy every day, she would improve ten times as rapidly. Tara adores him and worked so hard for him that he even changed her name from Ugly to Beautiful.

He seems to have a special knack for getting these children to perform at their peak, and Tara is no exception. When all else failed, and Tara began to balk, he threatened her with his "catastrophe," which he told her he kept locked in the closet. Tara didn't know what a "catastrophe" was, but it sounded horrible to her and the mere mention of it made her straighten up fast.

We were working in the new treatment and evaluation building, a large white structure with a huge room in the middle, surrounded by many little offices. It was in the big center room that we spent the week. All of the children who were there strictly for evaluation also waited in between appointments in the big room. Many of them came from foreign countries and didn't speak English. The various staff members got a big charge out of teaching Tara how to talk to the foreign children in their own language.

It was intensive therapy, all right, and Donna and I worked alongside the staff. Donna, who had to eat what was served in the dining room and was unable to control her salt intake, was experiencing a great deal of trouble with swollen ankles, legs, and hands. But that didn't keep her from working. I was trying to do most of the lifting and carrying for her and succeeded in throwing out my back. Between the two of us, we made a rather pathetic sight.

Somehow we managed to get through that rigorous week, and we were all pleased with the result of our efforts. First of all, we believed that Art really knew Tara and what she could and couldn't do. Therefore, we felt that the new program he administered was very well suited to her needs.

In addition, Tara had improved during the week. Her balance was much better, and she was sitting quite well. She seemed to have renewed energy to follow the program, too. We decided right then and there that we would always try to bring Tara for five-day appointments.

One of the things Art Sandler changed in Tara's program was the pattern itself. He said we had been giving in to her dislocated hip, which was very poor. In order to pattern her correctly, we would need four patterners instead of three. She was to receive thirty-two one-minute patterns a day, and these were to be performed very fast. Because Tara is so stiff, patterning her fast was nearly impossible. It required superhuman strength to do it. Donna's and my arms ached for days, and poor pregnant Donna was breathless from it most of the time.

If it was hard on us, it was equally hard on Tara. In the first place, it hurt her to have her body moved so quickly. As we moved her arms and legs, her body would literally be up in the air, and as we brought the arm and leg into position, her body would hit the table with a thud. Needless to say, she hated it, and screamed hysterically all the way through each pattern.

It hurt me to think that Tara spent thirty-two minutes a day screaming hysterically. One morning, a week or so after our return home, I had a long talk with Tara about her patterns.

"Maybe," I told her, "it would help if you asked Jesus to help it not to hurt and to help you not to cry."

She liked that idea, and began to ask God's help each time before she began a pattern. It worked, and she began crying less each time. Within a few weeks she was hardly crying at all.

Tara is very precise about her patterns and knows exactly how they are to be performed. Donna often says that Tara could teach her patterners their jobs single-handed, and I think she is probably right. One thing she is very particular about is where the lady who turns her head places her hands. She simply can't stand it if the patterner places her fingers too near her throat, and carries on almost hysterically, yelling, "I'm choking! I'm choking!" and gasps for air very convincingly.

In addition to the rigorous patterning, Tara was also repeating eighteen thirty-minute frequency sequences a day. She was still doing her upside-down hanging—this time with one person holding her legs apart and straight and one person pulling down hard on her hips, giving almost a traction-like effect. This was done for four minutes.

Then she grasped an overhead bar on her horizontal ladder with her hands, and, with the aid of volunteers, hung on and supported her weight for a minute. We were working on getting Tara to balance herself on her hands and knees during her sequences also. Another exercise was performed at the vertical ladder. Tara knelt on her knees, her bottom resting against her legs, and grasped an overhead bar on the ladder, then pulled herself up to a point where she was still on her knees but her legs were straight from the knees up.

She had a new piece of equipment called "The Turtle." This is rather like a low table on wheels. Tara is suspended underneath with a harness and is thus able to propel herself in a creeping motion on her hands and knees, without actually having to support her body herself. A kind neighbor of the carpenter who built this equipment painted a picture of a turtle on its tablelike top, which was a real thrill to

Tara. And, of course, there was the usual crawling and masking. We were instructed to mask Tara one hundred times each day.

It was during this difficult period that Tara started the practice of singing "Jesus Loves Me" during her patterns. As the women were struggling to move her stiff little arms and legs, and as Tara was struggling not to cry, she would sing in her loudest voice the comforting words, "Jesus loves me, this I know for the Bible tells me so. Little ones to him belong, they are weak but He is strong." This has remained her favorite patterning song, and she has since added a second verse. "I love Jesus does He know? Have I ever told Him so? Jesus likes to hear me say that I love Him every day." Recently, Tara was visiting a Sunday school class at a different church and was thrilled to be able to share her second verse to this well-known song with her new friends there.

10

Angel in Tennis Shoes

For months, we had been watching the progress of our new home, which was being built a mile away in a new section of Mission Viejo. Seeing our house being constructed was a fascinating if somewhat harrowing experience, but when moving day actually arrived, we were strangely unprepared.

While we were thrilled about our new home, we really hated to leave the old one. Donna and I stood in our empty living room that appeared so still and quiet now. We thought of how it had rung with children's laughter, and realized that someone else's children would laugh and play there.

We remembered our joy when Tara was born and thought of holidays and birthdays spent within these walls. And, of course, this home would always bring memories of that bleak time of Tara's accident. As we reflected on all the things that had happened to our family in this home, we wondered what might be in store for us in our new one.

Since we had no family nearby to help us, and the condition of my back and Donna's stomach left much to be desired, we decided to engage professional movers to handle the transfer of our furniture and personal belongings. We did all our own packing, though, and were fortunate in having the assistance of good friends. Several of Tara's patterners came over to help Donna pack and unpack kitchen supplies and to line cupboard shelves. Dick and Linda Payne, our sponsors at church and loyal patterners also, spent two whole days helping us to get settled and they even kept Mark and Tara overnight.

Our new home is nearly twice as large as our first one, and for weeks we just rattled around in it. The stairs required quite a period of adjustment and Donna, especially, had a hard time running up and down them all day. But we loved Tara's new workroom, which was more than twice as big as the tiny one she had used in the old house. She was very proud of it and showed it off to all her helpers. The change of homes seemed to have a stimulating effect on her and she worked much harder and with considerably more enthusiasm.

Now that we actually had a room for the nursery, Donna plunged into preparations for the new arrival. A dear friend, Bonnie Pope, had wallpapered one wall in a lime green, yellow, and orange print of castles and princesses and knights, and we painted the other walls lime green. The furniture would be white; some items were old, others were new, and most of the pieces had to be refinished. Donna spent most of her evenings out in the garage painting spindles on cradle and crib, and she had the nursery in perfect order with about two weeks to spare.

Knowing how busy she would be caring for an infant and patterning Tara, she had all clothing items stocked and ready, right down to the folded diapers and coming-home outfits. I teased her because she had two complete piles of clothes stacked on the changing table, ready for me to pick up the appropriate one to bring to the hospital. The blue ones were all hand-me-downs from Mark, but the pink ones were new.

Mark and Tara had both been born early, and we were expecting an early delivery this time also—especially since Donna had been experiencing false contractions for two months and engaged each day in rather strenuous physical activity. As April 5 came and went, we realized this baby had a mind of its own.

The children were growing more and more impatient, and so were we. Finally, on April 9, it began to look like the real thing. Donna patterned Tara right up to six o'clock that evening and can be proud that she didn't miss a single hour of Tara's program due to pregnancy through the entire nine months.

We had made previous plans to see a movie that night, and already had a sitter for the children. I was wary, but Donna insisted upon going anyway. She wouldn't even let me bring her packed suitcase along. I think she had practically given up hope that the baby would ever be born.

As we sat in the movie, I became more and more nervous. Donna usually had fairly short labors, and her contractions were coming closer and closer together. When they were two minutes apart, I put my foot down. She was going to that hospital whether she wanted to or not!

A quick check by the nurse confirmed that Donna was in first-stage labor.

"So you won't have to pay for an extra day, I'll wait until

midnight to officially admit you," she said as she led us to a labor room.

It was ten forty-five by now, and Donna and I settled down to watch television. We had taken natural childbirth classes together, and Donna was quietly making use of her breathing techniques.

All was going well, and about midnight Donna told me I really should ask the nurse to check her. After leisurely filling out admittance papers with me, the nurse ambled into Donna's room and found her still lying there quietly. However, examination revealed that the baby was nearly ready to be born. Accordingly, the nurse scurried out to call the doctor, who was still at his home nearby.

He arrived shortly thereafter and began to administer an anesthetic to numb the birth area. Donna was dutifully working on her part of the process when she became very sleepy.

"I'm so tired," she whispered. "I can barely keep my eyes open. I just can't push anymore."

Apparently, this was not what the nurse had expected to hear. She quickly checked Donna's blood pressure and then summoned the doctor. It soon became evident that Donna was experiencing an adverse reaction to the medication. The contractions came to a standstill, and Donna became numb all over. Her tongue was thick, her speech slurred.

"I can't feel anything anywhere and I can't move," she said. "Why can't I move? Why am I so sleepy? Something's not right!"

The nurse kept checking her blood pressure every few minutes, and the doctor was encouraging her to push. But it was hopeless. Donna couldn't make her body do anything. She was nervous, and she showed it. As for me, I was panic-stricken. Donna had always had very easy deliveries, but this time things were going wrong. What did it mean? What would happen? To Donna? To the baby?

It was hot and still, and I could feel perspiration trickling down my back. Donna was hot, too, and her short blond hair was as wet as if she had just washed it. Her face was flushed, her eyes darted about worriedly. Neither of us spoke the words, but we were both terribly frightened. What if all this caused brain damage in the baby?

"Oh, God, no!" I kept repeating silently over and over again. "We can't handle three brain-injured children! And yet, even so, Lord, Your will, not mine."

Donna, who had been wide awake and enjoyed watching the birth of both Mark and Tara, was drifting in and out of awareness, struggling to keep her eyes open and losing the fight most of the time. She had spent nine months convincing me how wonderful it was to witness the miracle of birth and had finally talked me into staying in the delivery room to share with her this precious moment.

But this seemed more like a nightmare to me. Donna had been unable to push the baby out, so the doctor went in with forceps to take it. My mouth was dry and I held my breath as I watched him pull out a purple, lifeless form. I gasped as I noted that the umbilical cord was wrapped around the baby's neck. I bit my tongue, thinking of Curt and Christie and the countless other children we knew who had been brain-injured through strangulation by the cord.

Donna was frantic. "Why isn't my baby crying? It's born! Why isn't it crying? What's wrong?"

One, two, three minutes went by. It seemed like forever. The doctor was patting and prodding. He finally pinched the still little figure on its bottom and it let out a lusty cry. I wiped my forehead, still shaking.

"What is it?" Donna was asking.

"A girl!" I choked.

"Oh–h–h–h. What color hair does she have?" Donna's voice was weak.

"It's light, kind of sandy-colored," I told her.

"A little girl with blond hair," Donna repeated incredulously. "Just what I wanted." I don't think she knew whether to laugh or cry.

My mind was reeling as I drove home in the early hours that morning. We had a baby girl. But was she going to be all right? What would we do if she wasn't? I tried to turn it all over to God, but it wasn't easy. My haggard face shocked Margo, who had come over to relieve our sitter around midnight. She had expected a proud new father and had gotten a worried one instead.

She notified the prayer chain at our church, and both Donna and I could feel the strength of their prayers. Mark was waiting up for me, too, huddled on the couch in his pajamas.

He had awakened for a drink around two a.m. and when Margo told him where we were he was too excited to go back to sleep. He was so thrilled about the baby that I wondered if I would ever get him to bed.

I had barely fallen asleep when it was time to get up again. Mark had to be taken to school and Tara had her therapy to do. Our wonderful patterners would continue to carry out her program while Donna was recuperating.

It was quite a shock when I went into Tara's bedroom to dress her and didn't find her there. It was the oddest feeling; I really didn't know what to think. Then I heard her little voice calling me from the nursery. Now I was really puzzled.

There she was, lying in the baby crib.

"Tara! What are you doing in here?" I asked, wondering if I were seeing things.

She grinned. "I told the baby-sitter this was my bed and my room."

"You're kidding!"

"No, I really did." she said. "At first he didn't believe me, but I convinced him." Her eyes were bright with mischief.

I gathered her in my arms and held her tightly. "Tara," I began, "Mommy had our baby last night—a baby girl."

She began squealing with delight and wiggling all over with excitement. "A baby girl? Just what I wanted! I didn't want an ugly old boy! What a wonderful God to give us a baby girl."

I took Donna's suitcase to her and was relieved to find her looking well. Her paralysis was totally gone, although it had lasted eight hours. She had seen the obstetrician and the pediatrician already, and both had reassured her that the baby was in good health. In fact, Donna had already been given an opportunity to feed her. Her eyes shone as she told me about our new daughter, whom we had named Christa Briana. She was a fine, strong, healthy baby—the largest of our three, weighing 8 lb. 7 oz., and measuring 20" long. She was equipped with all the necessary fingers and toes and had cute little ears and big blue eyes.

"And Michael," Donna bubbled, "her eyelashes and eyebrows are white. I think she's going to be very blond. You know how happy you are when somebody gives you a surprise present?" she continued. "And what if you unwrap it and find out that it's exactly the thing you've been wanting and praying for. Well, that's the way I feel about Christa. God has given us a wonderful surprise package that contained the very thing we wanted right down to the most minute detail."

Our patterners and churchwomen, under the direction of Wilma Chain, arranged to bring lunch and dinner to our home for ten days following Christa's birth. It was such a great help to us, and it was wonderful to realize that we had such good friends.

Donna's mother was expected to visit us from Texas, but was unable to come until the baby was ten days old and then could stay only three days. We had decided that we simply couldn't afford a baby nurse or any extra help when Donna came home from the hospital, and were concerned about how we would manage.

But, as always, God richly provided us with all our needs. I had recently become good friends with John Hobbs, a fine young man from Minnesota. Through him, we had met his sister Mary Gail, who is an aspiring actress. And it was Mary Gail who came to our aid at this time.

A strikingly attractive girl with long chestnut hair and flashing brown eyes, she seemed the least likely candidate for a baby nurse. But she loves babies and children in general and immediately fell in love with Christa and Tara—and Mark in particular. She worked with Tara during the day and kept Donna company; she even got up with Christa for the night feedings!

Every now and then, God gives us a very special friend—probably not more than one or two in a lifetime. Donna and Mary Gail have formed such a close friendship and it has been a real blessing to each of them.

On the night we brought Christa home from the hospital, we had a big birthday party for her. It was complete with cake and ice cream, and gifts for the three children. We brought the baby to the table in her infant seat and lit three candles on the cake because she was three days old. Then we all sang happy birthday to her and welcomed her into our family and into our hearts. As I looked around at the shining faces of my loved ones, I had to blink back tears of pure joy that God had given me such treasures.

Mark and Tara were delighted with their baby sister. They just couldn't get over how tiny she was, and actually fought over which one was going to hold her and feed her.

"She's my baby sister," Mark would say.

"No! She's *my* baby sister," Tara would shriek, and they would be at it again.

Donna allowed herself two weeks of respite from Tara's program, and then launched into it again. Unfortunately, Tara won't work as well for anyone else as she will for Donna, so Donna decided she had to get back to work just as soon as possible.

We marveled at how well we were able to manage with a baby in the house. Everyone had laughed at Donna when she told them the baby was going to be on a schedule. But when she told people that she had the routine made out before Christa was even born, that was just too much to accept. But, really, there wasn't any other way to do it.

When Christa ate, someone would have to take Donna's place, in working with Tara. In order to have people scheduled to take her place, Donna had to know exactly when Christa would be eating. So she had made out a routine for her. Christa would be fed at 8:30 A.M., 12:30 P.M., 4:30 P.M., 8:30 P.M., 12:00 midnight, and 4:30 A.M., as a newborn.

But Christa was such a good baby that by the time she was two weeks old she had abandoned the 4:30 A.M. feeding, and when she was three weeks old we were able to eliminate the midnight feeding also. By the time Christa was two-and-a-half-months old, she ate only three times a day, just like everyone else. She had breakfast at 9:00 A.M., lunch at 1:00 P.M., and dinner at 6:30 P.M.

One day, shortly before Christa was born, I was having my weekly meeting with Dr. Schuller regarding the various activities on which we were working together. As usual, he asked about the family, and naturally inquired about Tara. At that time I mentioned to him that Donna and I had long felt that God wanted us to write a book about her. Dr. Schuller had never seen Tara, but her story fascinated him, and he asked if he might come to our home to meet her.

It was arranged that I would drive him down the next afternoon. As I drove, I wondered what he would think of our little girl. Her room was full of patterners, as usual, with Tara perched on top of the big yellow-and-orange pattern table. She was dressed in a lavender body suit with matching ribbons tied around her long ponytails.

The Institutes required that she wear boys' high-top tennis shoes for part of her program, and the only ones we had been able to find were black. For therapy purposes, they had to be three sizes larger than her feet, and these heavy black masculine-looking shoes were in direct contrast to Tara's extremely feminine beauty. Donna and I often called her our "angel in tennis shoes" and this particular afternoon she looked very deserving of that nickname.

Tara flashed Dr. Schuller one of her dazzling smiles when he entered the room, and I knew she had gained another devoted follower. They were just getting ready to begin a pattern, and Donna invited Dr. Schuller to watch. As the women began this grueling ordeal, Tara launched into her favorite song, "Jesus Loves Me," and everyone joined in.

Tara insists that everyone sing with her and woe be to the person who has forgotten the words!   .

The faith of our little warrior made quite an impression on Dr. Schuller, and he asked to take my favorite photograph of her back with him to his office. The next Monday morning we were surprised to hear that he had devoted a portion of his Sunday sermon to Tara, and had used the picture. We could hardly wait until May 6, when the program would be aired on television.

Of course we notified our friends and relatives across the country, and all eyes were glued to the set that day. What a thrill it was to realize that Tara's story could bring inspiration to countless thousands through the miracle of television. We wondered what Tara would think about her television debut, and hoped it wouldn't affect her adversely. We needn't have worried.

After the program was all over, she looked thoughtful for a moment and then said, "How could I be on television and be here at the same time?" With that, as far as she was concerned, the subject was closed.

Two weeks later, Donna discovered a lump on Christa's arm. It was between the elbow and the shoulder of her left arm and was about the size of a large pea. Naturally, our doctor was out of town, so we had another doctor check her. We half-expected him to dismiss it as a fatty tumor, but he didn't. Its shape was irregular, and it was comparable to the size of a quarter in an adult's arm.

The doctor really wasn't sure what it was and thought that it should be removed immediately so a biopsy could be performed. He scheduled Christa for surgery two days later. Those two days were pretty nerve-racking. Surely, God wouldn't take our baby away from us, we thought. But what if Christa had cancer? She was only six weeks old, but we had all grown to love this tiny blond bundle. As we had done so many times before, we committed Christa and her tumor to the Lord, and asked that His will might be done. All we desired for ourselves was that He might give us a sense of peace about it and grant us strength to bear whatever the outcome might be.

Because she was so young, they decided not to put Christa in the hospital but to perform the operation in the doctor's office. They would administer a local anesthetic and strap her in a plastic infant form. The doctor reassured us, saying it was a simple procedure that would only take fifteen minutes.

Donna and I sat in the small waiting room and tried to read magazines. Actually, most of the time was spent in prayer. God had granted our request and had given us a sense of peace regarding our baby. Stark terror was replaced by gentle concern. I must admit, though, that when the fifteen minutes stretched into thirty minutes, I began to feel a little uneasy. What was going on in the doctor's office, anyway?

In reality, the surgery required forty-five long minutes. The doctor and the two nurses looked totally exhausted as they carried our little bundle from the room.

"It's okay," the doctor managed a weak smile. "The tumor is benign—just a little lipoma."

"Oh, dear God, thank you!" my heart sang. What a relief! Little Christa wasn't even fussy after her ordeal, and today she has only a tiny scar on her arm as a reminder.

As May lapsed into June, I got very busy. As a fireworks salesman, this was my most hectic time of year, and for months the tempo had been building. I had been working four nights a week since January, and had added Saturdays and Sundays to my work schedule in April.

It was a horrible job for any man with a family; and for a man with a family such as mine, it was really impossible. Each year I resented more and more the time spent away from Donna and the children. And how unfair it was to expect Donna to shoulder such a huge burden all alone. Mark especially needed his father. Here I had a beautiful new daughter, and I had barely seen her. For some time, I had been praying for a new job that would allow me to spend more time with my family.

One day, as I was meeting with Dr. Schuller, it looked as if my dream could become a reality. He offered me a full-time job with comparable salary and no night work! It would be an important move for our family, and Donna and I prayed about it for two weeks before coming to a decision. We truly felt that God had called me to this new position, and it was wonderful to think that I could be serving the Lord full time.

On June 15, I accepted the position as Dr. Schuller's executive assistant and planned to begin work on September 15.

It was about this same time that we received another pleasant surprise. Tara was going to be five on July 2, and while she had been toilet trained by day for two years, she had yet to stay dry during the night. Realizing that this was a problem with many brain-injured children, we weren't particularly upset by it. But we had set July as NDN day (no diapers at night). After all, a five-year-old was just too big for diapers. We were secretly dreading changing wet sheets each morning, however.

One night, a few weeks before Tara's birthday, we had company for dinner. I put Tara to bed without her diapers, thinking Donna could put them on when she went to tell Tara good night. But when she went up a few minutes later, Tara was sound asleep and looked so peaceful that she hated to wake her. The diapers were left off and the next morning, to everyone's amazement, Tara was dry! And she has been dry ever since. What a thrill it is to know that Tara has gained control over yet another part of her body.

Tara had her very first real birthday party that year, and it was the first time she actually had any friends to invite. We held it at Old McDonald's Farm, a lovely amusement area near our home, with many farm animals and pony rides. She was so excited that day, her little face just shone. Mary Gail and her good friend Casey MacDonald came down to help and took lots of pictures. They even made a tape recording of the affair for posterity!

Six months had elapsed since Tara had last been evaluated at the Institutes. She was due there on July 13. This would be an especially exciting visit, because Dr. Schuller would be coming with us. He was anxious to meet the people who exhibited such faith in brain-injured children.

My sister Gale had agreed to care for Mark, and Linda Payne would take Christa. It was surely hard to drag Donna away from that sweet little baby, but she finally consented to leave her. This would be another vigorous five-day appointment, and, as the big jet made its way across the country, Donna and I were lost in thought. Would Tara show as much progress during this visit as she had during the last? Little did we realize the exciting things that were in store for us in the week ahead.

11

Life Plan

The flight went smoothly, aside from several trips to the rest room with Tara. I have yet to figure out why she deems it necessary to visit the little girl's room so many times during an airplane flight. I think she uses this trick to ward off boredom. At any rate, I usually wind up feeling that I have walked all the way to Philadelphia.

We were met by the expected blast of hot, damp air in Philadelphia and scurried into the station wagon I had rented, thankful for air conditioning. The familiar route led us north to Fort Washington, just across the Philadelphia city limits, and we greeted the Sheraton Penn-Pike Hotel as one greets an old friend.

Lee and Dave Bulfin had driven down from New Jersey to spend the weekend, and we met them for dinner in the hotel dining room. Tara was pushed up to the table in her wheelchair and engaged in her favorite mealtime activity, which consisted of pulling everything within reach off the table and onto the floor. Lee and Donna and I realized that Tara had been unable to perform this mischievous feat when we had last seen them in January. It's funny how we wait for some improvement in function, and when it finally comes we immediately begin to take it for granted.

The next day was sheer joy for us—twenty-four hours with nothing to do! We slept late, an unspeakable luxury in itself, and drove out into the lush green Pennsylvania countryside. Dave's sister and brother-in-law live in a restored grist mill that was built in 1708, and we had been invited there for a picnic.

Located on eighteen acres of land, complete with a large pond (in California we would have called it a lake) and ducks, this estate was a child's delight. Tara fed the ducks bread, and they flocked around her and ate right from her hands. A tire hung suspended from a rope tied to an old elm tree, and I pushed Tara as she swung back and forth in it, her laughter echoing through the trees.

Later that day we were treated to an old-fashioned block party at the home of the Chains in Ardmore. Food-laden tables lined the street as neighbors gathered to enjoy the summer twilight. Tara, all smiles, was visiting with the children she had come to know during our many trips there.

In the manner of all good things, this free day was over too soon, and we found ourselves once more at the Institutes. They had opened a new building—the mobility center— since our last appointment and this was where we were scheduled to spend the week. In addition to Tara, there were fourteen other profoundly injured children who would be undergoing intensive therapy there.

This was Art Sandler's department, and he was racing

from room to room at a frantic pace. Each room held different pieces of equipment, and we were ushered into the one filled with overhead and vertical ladders. We knew that most of the families from California would be there, and had hoped that Tara would be working with children and parents we knew.

However, the frail little girl hanging from one of the ladders was new to us. We soon learned that her name was Nancy Rose, that she was eight years old, and that she lived in Indiana. She was stiff, like Tara, and I noticed from her uneven knees that she also had a dislocated hip. Unlike our healthy Tara, she was extremely thin and pale and acted rather listless. Due to lack of muscle control in the mouth area, she drooled and was unable to speak, although she could do advanced algebra and had an IQ in the genius range.

Nancy and Tara took an immediate liking to each other and enjoyed working side by side during the week. Because of their dislocated hips, they spent a lot of time doing the same exercises. Tara would look over at Nancy and smile, saying, "I just love Nancy. She's so cute."

Dr. Schuller, never having been exposed to brain-injured children before, was a little awestricken, I think, and sat quietly on the sidelines, deep in thought. After some discussion with Carl Delacato, the director of the Institutes' reading center, Dr. Schuller spent the remainder of the day with Glenn Doman, director of the Institutes.

As I had suspected, these two brilliant men developed an instant rapport and launched immediately into a lengthy discourse that lasted all day. I was fortunate enough to be able to sit in on a good deal of it; but most of their conversation, I must admit, went right over my head.

I periodically went over to the mobility center to check on

Tara, who was getting the workout of her young life. She and Nancy had been joined by three other children who had dislocated hips, and they were all hanging upside down by their good legs while their mothers manipulated their bad legs in a most gruesome manner. It was obviously a painful procedure, because the children were all screaming bloody murder. They spent the entire day repeating this sequence of hanging for four minutes and resting for two minutes.

Donna and Tara were both pale that night, the color having been literally drained from their faces. Tara's arms and legs quivered uncontrollably from the regimen of violent exercise, and her eyes were red and swollen from crying all day. Indeed, even the stoic Donna was on the verge of tears, brought on by physical and emotional exhaustion. I'm afraid that spending the day in a small room full of screaming brain-injured children is not her idea of a good time.

I put them both in a relaxing tub of hot water and ordered them a steak from room service. They were both in bed asleep by seven-thirty, when Dr. Schuller and I had to catch a plane for Washington, D. C. Here was the climax of eight months of work.

Tuesday we delivered twelve thousand letters to the Russian embassy, asking that they release the forty pastors who are imprisoned in Russia for preaching the Good News of Jesus Christ.

Meanwhile, Donna and Tara were hard at work. They had met Alan, a young high school student who was working at the Institutes during the summer. He was quite taken with Tara and was a big help to Donna in my absence. He even took Tara for a walk to look for wild blackberries during her lunch hour.

Dr. Schuller had been able to arrange some appointments in Washington for Wednesday, so I left him there and returned to Philadelphia alone. I arrived just in time to put my frazzled Donna and Tara into bed again.

The next day was especially exciting for Donna and me. Art and his staff worked with Tara and the other children while we parents spent the day in the auditorium listening to lectures. The highlight of the day was the Life Plan presentation given by Glenn Doman.

He explained that all children should have a plan for their lives. We all have plans for our well children. No one would think of letting his child grow up without some kind of plan for his future. It naturally follows that, if well children have plans, hurt children should also have plans. In fact, he asserted, hurt children need plans even more than well ones.

Most parents like to make big plans for their children; they want their children to reach the height of their potentialities. In this day and age, parents often set a goal of university graduation for their child. The lives of brain-injured children, however, are usually not planned, except in negative terms.

We tend to ask ourselves such questions as, "What are we going to do when she's too big to carry? What will happen to her when we're too old to care for her?"

According to Glenn Doman, we should set the same goals for our hurt children as we set for our well ones. The main consideration is that Tara should not become something simply because she couldn't be anything else. If we want our well children to be university graduates, we should want our hurt children to do as well. If our goal for our well children is that they be unskilled laborers, we should certainly want no less for our brain-injured child.

Dr. Schuller often says, "Don't put a ceiling on God."

Glenn Doman says, "Don't put a ceiling on your brain-injured child. It is better to aim for the university and fail than to aim for the institution and succeed. Our objective is to get all our kids into the university. But we will fail; we will fail over and over again. Of course, a good way never to fail is to never have objectives. In setting high objectives, we are certain to get higher results than if we set low objectives; even if we never completely reach the high objectives we have set for ourselves." He paused, then added: "I'm not promising you anything but trouble."

With this in mind, the Institutes has set up a series of "no later than" dates. Far from being an unrealistic set of impossible promises, these dates actually draw a circle around reality. For Tara, they set the goal of her eventual graduation from a university in June 1990 at the age of twenty-two.

Donna and I feel this is an excellent goal—one we would want for all of our children. But it is not the ultimate goal we would choose for them. We would want, in addition, that they be able to marry and raise healthy children, that they be sufficiently developed to be able to be good marriage partners and good citizens of our country. We would hope that they would be well-adjusted, happy individuals with much to offer others. It is this dream that we are working toward for Tara—and for Mark and Christa, as well.

The Institutes has devised a set of dates by which Tara must be able to function in a certain way in order to be able to achieve this goal.

In September 1986, when she is eighteen years old, Tara must enter the university if she plans on graduating in 1990. Prior to that, Tara must graduate from high school in June of 1986 in order to enter college that fall. Of course, in the first place, Tara must be totally well by the age of fourteen so that she can enter a normal classroom and attend high school.

Tara is currently, at five years of age, a normal child in every way with the exception of the two areas of mobility and hand function. Her visual, auditory, tactile, and language areas are not of vital concern to us, because she should continue to develop properly in these areas.

In having the goal of Tara being totally well by August of 1982 at fourteen years of age, we must have fail-safe dates by which she must accomplish certain things.

Her manual competence is very poor. She is operating at only the two-and-a-half-month level, having the ability to open her hands and release objects that could be hazardous to her. We hope that she will reach the next level, that of prehensile grasp, sometime soon. However, it can take her as long as five years to achieve this before it would be too late for her to continue toward her goals at the desired rate.

Prehensile grasp is the first grasp of babies, that of scooping with the thumb and all four fingers. After that, Tara must have cortical opposition—the ability to pick up objects with thumb and forefinger—in at least one hand by the time she is eleven. At twelve, she must have cortical opposition in both hands and be able to do it with both hands simultaneously.

By the time Tara is thirteen, she must have achieved the ability to use both hands well, but must have one hand in a dominant role. This means she must be either right-handed or left-handed. Her goal, then, at fourteen, is to be able to perform that most coordinated and uniquely human of all hand functions. She must be able to write with the hand that is consistent with her dominant hemisphere. In any totally organized human being one side of the brain is dominant.

This is called the individual's dominant hemisphere. If the left side of his brain is dominant, then he should be right-eyed, right-eared, right-handed, and right-footed.

If at any time, Tara reaches one of these dates and is unable to function at the appropriate level, then we will know we are failing to reach our goal. At that moment, we leave reality and enter a dream world until such time as we can bring her back to the development stage where she belongs.

Tara is now able to crawl on her tummy across the floor. In order for her to progress to her ultimate goal, she must be able to creep on her hands and knees by the age of ten. At the age of eleven, she must be walking as babies do, her arms in the air. At the age of twelve, Tara must be walking and running in complete cross-pattern—that is, with the opposite arm and leg moving together. This would hopefully enable her to use a leg in a skilled role, which is consistent with her dominant hemisphere by fourteen years of age. This means, for example, kicking a ball with her right foot, since she is right-sided.

When she can do all these things, she will be totally well.

The program at the Institutes may be unable to help her completely to achieve this miraculous goal. If not, we will certainly look elsewhere. There is the surgical work that Dr. Irving Cooper is doing. Perhaps we may eventually look into the possibilities of acupuncture. One thing is certain, however. We are not going to give up until every possible avenue for cure has been exhausted.

We have no guarantee that Tara will ever be well, although we pray earnestly that someday she will be. This is not up to us to decide. It is also not for the Institutes to decide. God also has a wonderful plan for Tara's life. It is an eternal plan far more wonderful than any we could devise; and much as we hate to admit it, it may not include Tara getting well at all. It is good to know that He will give us the courage to live out His plan, whatever it may be.

It was early evening by the time we left the auditorium. Ordinarily, ten hours of lectures would be a harrowing experience, but we were full of enthusiasm and energy. I'm afraid I can't say the same for the children, who were sprawled in an exhausted heap on the floor.

The following day brought more hard work. Art was trying to get Tara to stand up in the corner, and she was trying valiantly to oblige. It was especially difficult for her to stand up straight. Her legs wanted to bend at the knee. Art told her that her legs were an elevator.

"Come on, elevator, take me up to the penthouse," he would say in his strong eastern accent.

Tara was enchanted with this idea, and did her best to straighten her legs to make the "elevator" go up. After several times, she began to look puzzled.

"Art," she asked, "what's a penthouse?"

After having it explained that it was a beautiful apartment way up high, with a view of the city, where pretty girls lived and entertained their boyfriends, Tara was content to get back to work.

As she fought to keep her legs straight, Tara would say, "Come up to my penthouse. I'm going to cook your dinner and sing you songs."

Art winked at me. "You'd better not tell your daddy about that, pretty girl," he said.

Then he took us into another room that housed a large staircase covered with shag carpeting. "We're going to have Tara crawl down the stairs," he said. I looked up to the top of that tall flight of stairs. "Surely he doesn't mean all the way from the top," I thought to myself.

But that is exactly what he meant. I carried Tara to

the top and put her on her tummy, head first. Then I sat next to her and kept my hand on her back, just in case. To my surprise, Tara made it all the way down the entire flight of stairs in a matter of seconds. Breathless, but pleased, she begged to do it again.

The next day, when Art gave us our program for the ensuing four months, going down the stairs was one of the exercises to be repeated in Tara's frequency sequence. Once again, I was struck by God's guiding hand. The one thing that had bothered us about our new home had been the stairs. But if we had still been in a one-story structure, we would have had to build a staircase so that Tara could perform this exercise.

We left Philadelphia that Friday evening and flew to Houston for a thirty-six-hour visit with Donna's parents. Most members of the family hadn't seen Tara since her visit the previous summer and so could really see how much better she was at crawling and sitting.

When we boarded the airliner to return home, we realized they had mistakenly given us seats in the smoking section of the plane. We asked to be moved because cigarette smoke is not good for Tara. However, the flight was full and there were no other seats available for us in the coach. The stewardess then made arrangements for us to travel in first class, which had some seats left in the no-smoking section.

Donna and I had never flown first class before, and didn't really know what to expect. It was quite a pleasant surprise to us when the stewardess set our flight trays with linen tablecloths and complete china and silver service. Tara didn't notice. She was still sobbing unhappily over having to leave her grandparents.

As they began to serve the first course of our lunch, I

settled down in anticipation of a relaxing trip. A small voice at my side brought me back to reality.

"Daddy, I need to go potty."

I could immediately see the disadvantage of first-class service. Instead of being able to lift the meal tray off as I was accustomed to doing in coach, I had to empty my table, piece by piece. First the crystal glasses, then the several pieces of silverware, the little salt and pepper shakers, the hors d'oeuvre plate, and the napkin were all put in between Tara's and my seats. I picked her up and began my customary walk down the aisle to the tiny lavatory. How I manage Tara inside one of those minute compartments is a story in itself!

We returned to our seats, and I carefully reset my tray table again. No sooner had I put a few bites of my now-cold appetizer in my mouth, before Tara was at it again.

"I need to go potty, Daddy," she murmured, those big blue eyes looking up at me, the picture of innocence.

Off came the crystal, the silver, the salt and pepper shakers, the plate, and the napkin, and Tara and I took another walk. I wish I could say otherwise, but the truth is that Tara played this game with me all the way to Los Angeles. Donna, who was sitting across the aisle from us hooking a rug and reading the Bible, gave me sympathetic glances every now and then.

As the plane began its descent into Los Angeles, the attractive older woman who had been seated behind Donna came forward and began to speak with her.

"Did I hear you say you were taking a Golden West flight?"

"Yes," Donna answered.

"Are you by any chance going to Orange County?" she continued.

"Why, yes, we are," Donna said, quite puzzled by now.

"There is a company courier waiting to take my husband and me home to Newport Beach. We'd be glad to take you home. It would be so much easier for your daughter," the woman said.

Of course we were delighted and accepted her kind offer immediately. Sure enough, there was a station wagon with a uniformed driver waiting for us at the curb just outside the building. We soon learned that we had been befriended by none other than Walter Burke, the president of McDonnell-Douglas Aircraft Company.

They were quite interested in Tara. Mr. Burke, far from being a mere titular head of this famous corporation, was actually a scientist who had played a major role in designing our nation's spacecraft. He perceived immediately that gravity was Tara's worst enemy.

"She should be on the moon," he said. "Imagine all the things she would be able to do there, with its limited gravitational force."

I told the Burkes about the Institutes and what they were trying to accomplish for brain-injured children.

"Glenn Doman, its director, is going to be here in Los Angeles tomorrow to meet with my new boss, Dr. Schuller," I ventured. "Perhaps you would like to meet him."

"I'd like that," Mr. Burke said.

And so it was arranged. My mind was spinning. To think that these three dynamic men were brought together through our Tara.

After we had been home for a few minutes, I turned to Donna. "You know, this is all a part of God's plan. He wanted us to meet the Burkes and tell them about all the Taras in the world. God knew that the Burkes would be sitting in first class, so he managed to get us there, too!"

I don't think the world has yet seen the far-reaching implications that could come out of that meeting of three great minds.

As always, after a trip to Philadelphia, we were anxious to see Mark. Gale and Jack brought him down the afternoon we arrived home. His face lit with summer's glow, he proudly displayed the shells he had gathered on the beach.

This time we had yet another child we had missed. Donna, especially, could hardly wait to see Christa. She looked as though she had grown during our absence, and she recognized us, holding her little hands out for Donna to pick her up.

What a joy it has been to watch Christa grow and develop. It is truly a miracle to watch a baby learn; things seem to come so easily. After witnessing Tara fight and struggle for years to master a simple feat such as sitting up, it seemed odd to see a tiny six-month-old baby sit with such ease and grace.

Though we are delighted that Christa can do these things, it makes us doubly sad that Tara can't. Tara, however, doesn't seem to mind that her baby sister is passing her by in terms of achievement. She and Mark are very proud of Christa's accomplishments. For months they have held her and repeated over and over, "Say da-da, Christa. Say da-da."

If Christa happened to let out a baby "ahh," they would both squeal in delight. "She did it! She did it! Christa said da-da!"

A few weeks later, our family had the extreme pleasure of spending a week at Forest Home Christian Conference Center, a wonderful nondenominational retreat camp located in our local San Bernardino mountains. The fresh air and friendly atmosphere did us all a world of good and, as usual, our Tara was an inspiration to many of the campers there.

During one of the evening meetings, the director of Forest Home, the Reverend Stanley Collins, was addressing the gathering.

"I know sometimes people wonder why God doesn't heal them when they are seriously ill or disabled. They worry that maybe their faith isn't strong enough. However, the Bible makes it very clear that God heals people to bring Himself glory. It also makes it clear that sometimes He feels He can be glorified more by working through a person who is weakened by disease or handicap than by actually healing that person."

Donna and I practically jumped for joy, as did many of our friends who were seated around us. Here was what we had always felt God was doing with Tara, but we had never found the correct words to explain it before.

Our afternoons were free at camp, and Donna and I usually tried to nap for an hour or so. We wanted Tara to sleep, too, but she would have no part of it.

One day she wet her pants while we were resting, became extremely upset and began to cry. Half asleep, I staggered over to her bed, prepared to be very stern, when suddenly her tears turned to laughter. She began virtually wiggling for joy. "Jesus loves me anyway!" she exclaimed. "Even when I wet my pants! I'm so happy!"

While Tara had not changed much during her week at the Institutes this time, she made three startling improvements shortly thereafter. She learned to bring herself up almost to a sitting position from lying flat on her back. At the same time, she became able to sit alone for short periods of time with her legs straight out. Prior to this, she had been able to sit only in Indian style, with her legs spread for balance. Tara was also standing in the corner much better.

One day, as she was standing, her wobbly legs bending every now and then, she laughed, "I'm going up and down, just like a merry-go-round."

Now that she was five years old, the school district sent Tara a home teacher. Mrs. Flores was to come for an hour each day, five days a week, to teach her kindergarten. Tara was ecstatic. The first day Mrs. Flores was scheduled to appear, Tara could barely contain her excitement. She told everyone about it and kept asking when she was coming. When Mrs. Flores finally arrived, Tara was so thrilled she was stunned speechless. Her eyes grew as big as saucers, her mouth fell open, and she just stared, unbelieving.

Donna helped Tara to sit up Indian style, as Mrs. Flores explained that she would be giving Tara a developmental test in order to determine her capabilities, and indicated that Donna should leave them alone.

Donna was nearly as excited as Tara and couldn't drag herself completely away from the scene. As a result, she waited in the hall outside the workroom door and listened. Mrs. Flores explained the test to Tara, then launched into some questions.

"Tara, what flies?"

Tara was quiet for a moment, thinking. Then she said in her little voice: "Birds fly, and airplanes, and bees, and flies." And so they progressed through a series of additional questions that were part of the test.

A few days later, when Mrs. Flores gave Donna Tara's score, she was careful to explain that it was not entirely accurate. The exam had some manual parts to it, she said, and the scoring apparatus had no way of adapting itself to a child who couldn't use her hands. Therefore, Tara had received a zero for those portions of the test. However, despite that particular handicap, Tara had performed at a four-year, four-month level—just about the same as most "normal" children did upon entering kindergarten.

"I wish I had a whole classroom of children who were as enthusiastic about learning as Tara," she concluded.

A few days later, Tara was working hard crawling down the stairs when she moved her arm a little more awkwardly than usual and bumped her head on the next step.

"Ouch!" she said, wrinkling her nose. "That hurt my brain. I have a brain, you know. Everybody has a brain. Someday I'm going to learn to walk, and then I'm going to give my brain away." So much for five-year-old logic.

Donna and I always tuck our children into bed at night as a team. It is a special time, a quiet time. A time for secrets to be shared and questions to be asked and answered. We always wind up with a prayer—sometimes ours, sometimes theirs.

Mark holds the family record for the silliest prayer with this one he spun off at the age of three:

> Now I lay me down to sleep.
> I say my prayers,
> I go to sleep.
> I wet the bed.

But Tara's are by far the most poignant. She normally asks Jesus to help all the little children she has seen at the Institutes, naming them one by one. One night, at the end of her list, she added:

Dear God, please help me to
learn to walk so I can walk
to Your house.

"I love you, Mommy, I love you, Daddy. God bless you,"
she called as we walked from her room.

Donna and I blinked at each other through our tears. We
didn't speak, but we were each thinking the same thing.
How wonderful that God could turn such a hopeless tragedy
into such a great blessing.

Epilogue

Well, here we are in 1981. Where has all the time gone? Minute by minute, day by day, seven full years have passed since we finished writing Tara's book. The last chapter was about Tara's Life Plan—about the hopes and dreams and prayers we had for Tara's future.

She is thirteen years old now, and according to the Life Plan you have just read, she should be walking and running in complete cross-pattern and have cortical opposition in both hands. We set high goals for Tara—the highest—in the hope that if she didn't reach them she would at least be better off than if we had set no goals at all.

I am sitting here at my desk right now. A yellow lamp is casting light on the paper, and I hold a ball-point pen in one hand. The other hand is held tightly over clenched jaws and pursed lips, and there is a giant-sized lump in my throat. "How can I tell them, Lord?" I ask. "How can I tell them that we failed?"

I'm looking back over what I wrote so long ago. "If at any time, Tara reaches one of these dates and is unable to function at the appropriate level, then we will know we are failing to reach our goal." That, I suppose, is the beauty of definite goals. It is easy to see when you are failing to meet them.

And now I am looking at another paragraph from the past. "We have no guarantee that Tara will ever be well, although we pray earnestly that someday she will be. This is not up to us to decide. It is also not for the Institutes to decide. God also has a wonderful plan for Tara's life. It is an eternal plan far more wonderful than any we could devise; and much as we hate to admit it, it may not include Tara's getting well at all. It is good to know that He will give us the courage to live out His plan, whatever it may be."

The Bible tells us in the Book of Romans, chapter 11, verses 33 through 36, "Oh, what a wonderful God we have! How great are his wisdom and knowledge and riches! How impossible it is for us to understand his decisions and his methods! For who among us can know the mind of the Lord? Who knows enough to be his counselor and guide? And who could ever offer the Lord enough to induce him to act? For everything comes from God alone. Everything lives by his power, and everything is for his glory. To him be glory evermore."

And so, God is working out His plan. It is not the plan I would have chosen, nor do I pretend to understand it. It is not always an easy plan of which to be a part. In fact, sometimes it is extremely painful. But I can say in all honesty that God has been with us every step of the way. He has never, not once, left us alone in our situation, nor has He failed to compensate us in other ways for our struggles. God is faithful, and He is able to see us through all circumstances, no matter how difficult. And I am not just speculating. I know this is true. It is true that I believe it, but I have more than believed it—I have lived it.

In the past seven years, I have learned a lot about brain-injured children. One of the most important, and most tragic, things I have learned about them is that they often make dramatic strides in their young, formative years, only to lose part of what they have gained as they grow into maturity. It's almost as if the quest for normalcy, or at least the complete development of potential, were like a huge mountain to be scaled, and the brain-injured child were like "the little engine that could." He is the little, powerless engine with the big dream of making it up over the crest of the mountain.

At first the little engine huffs and puffs and tries and tries against seemingly impossible odds and keeps repeating over and over as it struggles hopefully along the track, "I think I can—I think I can." Sometimes the little engine is able to gather up enough momentum to reach the top of that great mountain peak and coast gracefully into the beautiful green, flower-strewn valley on the other side.

But other times, no matter how hard the little engine huffs and puffs, regardless of his optimism and the innumerable times he repeats, "I think I can," irrespective of how many spectators stand along the sides of the tracks to cheer him on, the little engine just can't get going fast enough to make it all the way to the top of such a formidable mountain. At times it may appear that he is going to do it, but in the end it becomes painfully obvious that he just isn't going to make it.

The main problem with this seems to be that there is no siding for the little engine to pull off onto for safety. And no matter how hard he hits his brakes, he reluctantly begins to slide back down the big mountain he worked so hard to climb. Naturally all those skeptics who had belittled the little engine's first attempts to climb the mountain are on hand, never missing an opportunity to say, "I told you so!" His friends and family stand behind the little engine, pushing and shoving with all their might to keep him from slipping. But eventually, they realize that it is hopeless. No matter how hard they try, they are just not strong enough to resist the gravitational forces that are continually pulling on the little engine. And if they persist in standing behind him, they realize that the little engine will accidentally run over them on his way down the mountainside.

And so they stand aside and watch in despair as they see the little engine that tried so hard begin to slip farther and farther back down the mountain. And they run along beside the little engine and call to him encouragingly. They try to find out the safest and easiest ways for a little engine to slide and do their best to teach them to the little engine. They make sure that the little engine has plenty of coal for his fire and water for his boiler. And, when they hear of a new route to the top of the mountain, they go exploring and take their tools and do their best to blaze a trail through the trees and lay some more track for the little engine.

Sometimes, it seems that the little engine may make some progress along the new track; but he just hasn't got the power. The momentum just isn't there. And so the little engine continues his slow descent, and he hopes, and his friends hope, that something wonderful will happen that will keep him from sliding all the way back down to the bottom.

This is pretty much where we are with Tara right now. Up until about the age of nine, she continued to make very slow but nevertheless steady progress, although she never came anywhere near the goals we had set for her in her Life Plan. Her highest achievement was that she began to make some progress in getting up on her hands and knees to creep. She never achieved any sort of hand function.

As the years passed, looking realistically at the goals she

failed to achieve and realizing Glenn Doman's words that these "no later than" dates actually draw a circle around reality, we came to the point where we had to come face-to-face with the harsh reality that Tara just wasn't going to make it to the top of her mountain. Her brain was too profoundly injured to respond properly to the programming we had given her. And it hurt—much more than words can say.

We didn't give up, though, even though we could see the handwriting on the wall. We kept trying, taking Tara to more specialists than I would care to remember. We tried chiropractic and acupuncture, entailing countless long freeway drives, day after day, for months on end. All to no avail.

Finally, at age nine, we decided to try the ultimate: a cerebellar stimulator. Popularly called a brain pacemaker, this incredible device was developed by Dr. Irving Cooper in New York and has achieved many miraculous results. It consists of an electrical implant placed at the base of the brain, on the cerebellum, underneath the skin at the base of the skull. From here, also under the skin, a wire runs down the neck which attaches to a receiving unit installed under the skin on the upper chest. An antenna is then placed over the receiver on the outside of the body which is connected by a long wire to a battery pack worn outside. The battery gives power to the receiver, which in turn transmits it to the implant, which then electronically stimulates the brain. The most publicized benefits of this device are decrease in spasticity, ever and always Tara's greatest problem, and reduction in seizure activity. We were interested in both, because earlier in the year Tara had suffered her first seizure since her original hospitalization following her accident.

Brain surgery: Somehow I had never thought of the implantation of the electrodes as brain surgery. Some of the material I had read on the subject had said it was no more dangerous than a tonsillectomy. We chose our surgeon carefully, and flew Tara back East in order to have a Christian doctor who believed in patterning.

Our month's stay there was completely devastating. The surgery took nine and one-half hours to perform. We were not pleased with the hospital's facilities. By the grace of God, Tara recovered, but the results were bitterly disappointing. We had hoped for improved function. There was none. She was a bit looser perhaps, with slightly improved eyesight. Nothing more.

After this last attempt at trying to change the brain directly, we began once more to explore orthopedic measures. Because of the enormity of Tara's spasticity problem, most doctors had always discouraged us from orthopedic surgery. Others had advised us to wait until Tara was a bit older, to give her a chance to mature and improve on her own before resorting to surgery. Well, we reasoned, Tara was older, and we had tried absolutely everything else known to medical science at this point in time. Surely now was the time for orthopedic surgery.

But we were destined once again for disappointment. The same doctors who had advised waiting now said it was too late. Tara was too old, too large, her spasticity too pronounced. It would be a waste of time. As one renowned orthopedic surgeon told us, "I can give Tara beautiful X rays, but her hips will probably still hurt and she will not have any improvement in function. Why put her through a serious, painful operation just so she can have good-looking X rays?"

We had to face the fact that, even though it is a brain-injured child's best friend, the rigorous patterning program had been unable to succeed with Tara. The brain pacemaker had failed; traditional physical therapists just shook their heads and spoke of teaching Tara to handle an electric wheelchair. Orthopedic surgery was useless, as was chiropractic and acupuncture. There was simply nothing left to try. This realization was slow in coming, more like a buildup over the years, but finally it was there. And it couldn't be ignored. Tara had gone as far up her mountain as she could go. And it is true that she was much farther up that mountain than she ever would have been had we given up in the beginning and never tried to reach the summit.

And we stood, precariously perched in the rock-strewn cliff near Tara's railroad tracks, about a quarter of the way up the mountain, and looked down over all the territory she had climbed. And we were proud of our little engine who had so heroically attempted to achieve the impossible. We were proud of every one of the achievements she had made on the way up, no matter how small they might seem to others. And we were grateful to God for giving us the strength and the courage to dare with Tara to dream the impossible dream.

In actuality, we hadn't failed at all. We had set out to help Tara reach her highest potential, and we had. It wasn't as high up the mountain as we had hoped, but it was as high as she was able to climb. She was our daughter, the little girl God intended us to have, and we loved her. We would never have to look at her and wonder whether she could have done better had we tried harder, for we had dug down deeper and given her more. And that knowledge alone is enough to bless us through all eternity.

Probably the most disconcerting event in Tara's life in

the past three years or so has been increased and persistent seizure activity. Although we had been thoroughly indoctrinated in the Institutes' belief that medication to prevent seizures is worse than the seizures themselves, there seemed to be little else we could do. They were so frequent and left Tara so exhausted that she was unable to do practically anything. Mike was distraught. I was distraught. So was Tara's teacher at school. But the seizures were harder on Tara than on anyone else. She could feel them coming and knew when they were over. And they terrified her. So we reluctantly began the rounds of neurologists and the experimenting with drugs. It took us nearly two years, but we finally got those seizures under control. Tara hasn't had one now in nearly a year, but she is under heavy doses of medication on a daily basis.

I don't know whether the seizures themselves further damaged the brain, or whether it is a side effect of the drugs, or a combination of the two. I only know that Tara is not the same child she was three or four years ago. Maybe the little engine is just too tired of trying so hard. At any rate, gone are the twinkling eyes, the boundless energy, the constant smile, the incessant chattering.

Nowadays Tara is mostly quiet. Her speech comes slowly and is not always organized well. She tires easily and often naps in the afternoons. But every now and then, the old fire returns to her lovely hazel eyes, and she laughs and talks and returns, if only briefly, to her old zest for life. Somewhere inside, Tara is still there. And who knows what miracle God might use to restore her completely?

Tara is a happy child, very sweet and exceptionally kind and thoughtful. She is very responsible and, if she could use her arms and legs, she would be perfectly capable of caring for herself and others. She would make an excellent baby-sitter, as she loves children and has a very good knowledge of right and wrong, safe and dangerous. Whenever there is a squabble among the children of our household, Tara can always be counted upon to give a reliable, true account of the actual circumstances. And she is an unusually caring, compassionate person, someone who really loves and feels deeply for others. In short, were it not for her extreme handicaps, she is precisely the kind of daughter you would love to have.

She goes to a nongraded public school in our area that is for children with orthopedic and multiple handicaps. There she struggles with reading and basic math facts, both of which are extremely difficult for her. She types at an electric typewriter using a headgear, and paints with her mouth. She spends most of her waking hours in a wheelchair, and longs for the day when Mom and Dad can get her an electric one that she can manipulate herself.

Tara's eyesight remains very poor. In fact, last year we learned that it falls within the limits of legal blindness. But even so, she sees well enough to have crushes on some of the more attractive currently popular rock 'n' roll singers. Music is still her first love. She is especially partial to vocal arrangements that she can sing along with.

As for our family, there are six of us now. Mark is fifteen, Tara twelve, Christa seven, and Shannon (another son) is four. Like Job, who was blessed with twice as many children as he lost, we have been given two wonderful, normal, healthy children since Tara's tragic accident. God is so good. In most ways, we are like any average family—we laugh and cry and play and fight together, but mostly we love. And the fact that Tara is brain-injured does not change her from being a much-loved daughter. A person's worth is not measured in what he can or cannot do, or in how he looks, or even in how he acts. Ultimately, a person has worth because he is created in the image of God, because he has an eternal soul, and because God loved him enough to become a man and die for the forgiveness of that eternal soul. In the scope of eternity, nothing else really matters.

Tara knows this and understands it. Recently, a little neighbor boy asked Tara when she was going to get well. Tara just smiled her sweet, peaceful smile and said, "When I get to heaven, then I'll be perfect." I don't think anyone on earth could ever boast of a more glorious future. That is true achievement of our highest potential.